The DAD Coach

ALSO BY THE AUTHOR

The Matheny Manifesto

The DAD Coach

How to Lead Kids to Succeed On and Off the Baseball Field

Mike Matheny

with Jerry B. Jenkins

CROWN
NEW YORK

CROWN
An imprint of the Crown Publishing Group
A division of Penguin Random House LLC
1745 Broadway,
New York, NY 10019
crownpublishing.com
penguinrandomhouse.com

Library of Congress Cataloging-in-Publication Data
Names: Matheny, Mike, 1970– author. | Jenkins, Jerry B., author. Title: The dad coach : how to lead kids to succeed on and off the baseball field / Mike Matheny, with Jerry. B. Jenkins. Other titles: How to lead kids to succeed on and off the baseball field Identifiers: LCCN 2024036409 (print) | LCCN 2024036410 (ebook) | ISBN 9780593442876 (hardcover ; acid-free paper) | ISBN 9780593442883 (ebook) Subjects: LCSH: Youth league baseball—Coaching. | Baseball for children—United States—Coaching. | Baseball for children—Training. | Sportsmanship. | Teamwork (Sports) | Interpersonal relations in children. | Motivation (Psychology) in children. | Determination (Personality trait) in children. | Perseverance (Ethics) | Time management.
Classification: LCC GV880.65 .M38 2025 (print) | LCC GV880.65 (ebook) | DDC 796.357/62—dc23/eng/20250108
LC record available at https://lccn.loc.gov/2024036409
LC ebook record available at https://lccn.loc.gov/2024036410

Hardcover ISBN 978-0-593-44287-6
Ebook ISBN 978-0-593-44288-3

Editor: Matt Inman | Assistant editor: Fariza Hawke | Production editor: Natalie Blachere | Text designer: Aubrey Khan | Production manager: Jessica Heim | Copy editor: Thomas Pitoniak | Proofreaders: Kimberly Hill and Jacob Sammon | Publicist: Tammy Blake | Marketer: Mason Eng

Manufactured in the United States of America

9 8 7 6 5 4 3 2 1

First Edition

The authorized representative in the EU for product safety and compliance is Penguin Random House Ireland, Morrison Chambers, 32 Nassau Street, Dublin D02 YH68, Ireland, https://eu-contact.penguin.ie.

To the memory of the epitome of coaches, John Wooden,
to whom character took precedence over ability.

And to the man who remains my own Dad Coach
to this day, Jerry Matheny.

Also to Kristin and our kids, their spouses,
and our grandchildren:

Tate and Margaret (Ryker, Gunner, and Rory),

Katie and Tyler (Jax and Shay-Mikey),

Luke and Annabella,

Jake and Macy (Asher),

and Blaise.

You bless me beyond my ability to express.

Also to my little band of Warriors who have become men.
Thank you for one of the best experiences of my life.

"Where one teaches, two learn,"
and I have learned so much from each of you.

Thank you for allowing me to be your coach.

Thank you to Steve Linton, John Mabry, and
Rick Sems for being great Dad Coaches and taking
over when I got called up to the big leagues.

I hope you take as much pride as I do
in what our boys accomplished.

A coach will impact more people in one year
than most will in a lifetime.

—BILLY GRAHAM

Contents

The DAD Coach

Introduction

Want to Make a Real Difference?

I'm guessing you're reading this book because perhaps you're desperate. You drew the short straw, or maybe in a moment of weakness volunteered to coach a youth-league baseball team. Whether or not your own son is on the team, if the kids you're to coach fall between the ages of six and twelve, my goal is to help you maximize your critical role.

If you're coaching six-to-eight-year-olds, you're likely involved in tee ball. Nine-and-ten-year-olds might make use of coach pitching or start having the kids on the rubber. Eleven-and-twelve-year-olds will, of course, be on their own on the field. Beyond that age, kids will often be trying out for advanced or traveling teams and looking to play high school ball.

Regardless of the age of your players, you might be tempted to view coaching as simply a civic duty, a diversion you might enjoy, something fun that you might even be good at. As a fan and maybe a former player, you know the basics, the ins and outs of the game, and maybe you even see yourself as a savvy strategist.

But now you find yourself with a dozen or more packages of

pure energy. Just keeping them in one place while they throw projectiles and swing clubs seems daunting. If you're not diligent about taking charge immediately, you could wind up with a bunch of kids at your feet, tackling each other in the outfield, throwing tantrums when they strike out. Then you might find yourself on the phone with parents who suggest better ways to train and use their sons. Believe me, I've been down this road, being the only big-league manager to come directly from coaching a youth-league team. So let me help you here.

Believe it or not, you have the real opportunity—and may I say a serious responsibility—to profoundly influence these potential world-changers. That may sound outlandish, but I'm a believer in youth sports and their ability to change lives. Sports made a colossal impact on me, but not for the reasons you might think. Yes, I became one of the very few kids who went on to become a college scholarship athlete, a Major League Baseball player, and eventually a manager, but I'm talking about an entirely different kind of impact.

The old-school coaching I was privileged to receive is not what made me a big leaguer. That was the result of physical and athletic gifts for which I can't take credit—though I don't apologize for exploiting them by striving to be the best I could be. Rather, the way I was coached molded me into the *person* I am today. It gave me the drive, the determination, the perseverance—which I contend would have blessed me with success in any life endeavor, even if I had not been fortunate enough to have been athletically gifted.

That's why I'm committed to seeing that kind of coaching become the norm again, to stop having to refer to it as some treasured relic.

Let me get right to my point: Too many parents who volunteer—

or are pressed into duty—to coach their kids' sports teams, begin with the wrong idea of success. It is well-documented that less than 1 percent of the kids they coach will play that same sport at even the varsity level in high school, let alone at the collegiate or professional level. Yet I see many youth-league coaches catering to that 1 percent.

I propose we use sports to teach young people not only the skills that can make them the best players they can be, but also the character qualities that can make them the best adults they can be. Better spouses. Better parents. Better professionals, leaders, teachers, executives, employees. Let's invest in young athletes during their most formative years to help them learn the power of teamwork, instill in them the pride that comes from hard work, teach them how to lose with dignity and win with respect—and develop the ability to go the extra mile, to persevere, and to effectively manage their time. All while establishing meaningful lifelong relationships.

If you're as fortunate as I have been, a decade or more down the line you'll look back on that first day and try to remember what the grown men you now know looked like, acted like, and sounded like when they first joined your team. To see these young men today and hear them recall what meant the most to them as teammates back when they were kids—well, it doesn't get better than that. I'll include several of their memories throughout, and if those spark in you a desire for the same kinds of results, I hope it makes you double down on a resolve to do this right. Sure, anyone would be thrilled to say they coached a kid to athletic greatness. But imagine playing a role in turning kids into people of true character.

Coaching done right can help raise great leaders, men and women capable of influencing every facet of our future world.

Your First Step

We'll start by examining your view of success. Once we're on the same page, I'll propose ideas, theories, and processes proven to help you navigate these strange waters. Along with some talented Dad Coaches, I have designed age-specific drills and exercises to develop skills and have drawn up step-by-step practice plans to help you achieve the improvement these young ballplayers hope to achieve. I'll offer game preparation and evaluation techniques to help keep you on track and the kids engaged. Fun should be the primary goal at the early ages, and I'll offer time-tested advice on how to make this not just an experience you endure, but also one of the most meaningful time investments of your life.

Why?

Because character development is even more important than athletic training.

Sure, you might become that rare coach who sees one kid out of a hundred thank you the day he wins a scholarship, or you might even see that one kid out of a million get drafted into the pros. Or not.

If you define success by that 1 percent, or worse, by that one-in-a-million, you're likely to be disappointed.

But get character development right and you'll have *all* the kids you coach, regardless of whether they ever play the game again, thanking you for teaching them life skills. You can't beat that.

If for you the definition of coaching success becomes instilling character into the 99 percent, you'll enjoy fulfillment that lasts a lifetime.

The Genesis of This Book

As I trudged off the field at Fenway Park in Boston in the fall of 2013, I felt dejected for the second time by a World Series. As manager of the St. Louis Cardinals, I had seen the Red Sox win the championship in six games.

I had to admit I'd come a long way since my last World Series appearance. That was in 2004, when I was a catcher with the Cardinals and the Red Sox swept us in four games. It had been a destiny postseason for Boston, during which they overcame a three-games-to-none deficit in the American League Championship Series against their rival New York Yankees. Beating us sent the World Series championship trophy home to Beantown for the first time in eighty-five years.

So, nine years later, I again found myself in that "so close, yet so far" abyss.

But what a ride to get to that point.

I had retired from baseball in 2006 after thirteen years as a catcher for four major-league teams. The next year, a group of parents of a ten-and-under youth baseball team (which included one of my sons) asked if I would become the coach. Frankly, part of me worried they just wanted to be able to say their kids were being coached by a former big leaguer. I was pretty sure they didn't realize how strongly I felt about coaching kids. I was willing to undertake this, but under several conditions I outlined in a five-page, single-spaced letter in response to their request.

I wrote it because I hadn't planned to coach a team. I would have been just fine sitting and watching the games from way down the right-field line. Youth sports had changed too much since my childhood days in Reynoldsburg, Ohio, riding my bike with my glove on the handlebars to JFK Park.

During the offseason I watched my kids play indoor soccer

and ice hockey, and it became obvious to me that some of the adults were absolutely off their rockers. I found unbelievable and downright wrong the craziness among parents in the stands and in the parking lots, and the way some coaches treated the kids.

So, I thought it best to be clear with the other parents about what I would expect if I were to coach a team. My wife, Kristin, and I invited them over, and I read them the letter—which hadn't seemed that long or that big a deal when I was writing it. It sounded much better in my head than it did in my living room in December 2007. The letter came across with much more edge than I intended. Here I was, basically scolding a group of very respectable, highly successful, intelligent people for offenses they hadn't even committed yet.

The gist was that youth baseball "is ALL about your son, not you. The best thing you can do is to hand them off to me and the other coaches and go sit silently and watch." I may have actually delivered it with a little more tact than that, but not much. I wanted to make abundantly clear that the definition of success in youth baseball had been radically skewed. Success was now defined by how many trophies a coach collected (only to find their place in the local landfill within a couple of years) or how much could be fleeced from parents for pitching, hitting, and fielding lessons; strength and speed training; and mental toughness sessions—for their seven-year-old! And the holy grail, the ultimate success? That ever-elusive full-ride scholarship.

Come on!

Suffice it to say, I finished reading my letter and saw a room full of ashen faces—including Kristin's.

But to my astonishment, this had resonated with them and they were in.

In fact, one of the parents—without my knowledge or permission—posted my letter on the internet, and it took on a life of its own. That's when I first became aware that something could "go viral." One of my fellow coaches jokingly referred to it as "The Matheny Manifesto," much to my embarrassment, and somehow that stuck. It seemed everywhere I traveled, someone had printed and tacked up my "manifesto" in a locker room or a gym or a dugout.

We had a great experience with that first baseball team and added a few more teams over the next few years. In 2012, I was hired as manager of the St. Louis Cardinals and enjoyed a bit of a honeymoon there the first few seasons.

I soon began hearing from authors lobbying to join me in writing a book based on that original letter, so I considered the viability of such a project. I had a good conversation about it with one of my favorite authors, Jerry Jenkins. He wasn't available at the moment, but I wasn't convinced anyway. I kept asking myself, *Who am I to write a book? What have I done to warrant it?* I didn't have a good enough answer yet.

Fast-forward to that pitiful walk of shame after another World Series loss in 2013. As I considered projects that might offer career purpose, I knew I needed to write the book based on the so-called manifesto. Too many people had told me the message was important and already impacting coaches, parents, and eventually kids. And that was through only word of mouth. I needed to set aside my misgivings and do what I believed to be right. Who knew how long I would enjoy the platform of being one of thirty people on the planet fortunate enough to manage a Major League Baseball team? It was time to act.

Kristin and I decided to take a step of faith and figure out how to get it done. Fewer than forty-eight hours later, I received an unsolicited email from Jerry Jenkins, telling me that he now believed we were meant to write that book together.

I still get chicken skin when I tell that story. I have never claimed to hear the audible voice of God or see any handwriting on the walls, but how hard do you need to be hit in the head to realize that something bigger, dare I say, someOne bigger, is at work here?

I am still blown away—and so grateful—that *The Matheny Manifesto* became a *New York Times* bestseller. Yet I've long felt that while it did its job of telling "what" coaches should do, it left a gaping hole of "how" they can do it. That's the reason for the book you're reading now. We wrote *The Dad Coach* to help you make the most of these irreplaceable years and opportunities.

I'm grateful that a slew of longtime friends and associates, who really know the game, have agreed to come alongside and share their knowledge with you. You'll find *The Dad Coach* chock-full of QR codes linking to videos that walk you through every concept I recommend.

Your goal should be to infuse your players with a love for the game, show them the value of bonds that will last far beyond their playing days, and reinforce character traits that will bode well for them in whatever profession they choose. So never apologize for making impact your goal.

What could be better than creating priceless memories and becoming a coach who models avoiding discord in your most precious relationships?

Baseball is our classroom. So stop asking, "Who am I?" and let's go make a real difference.

What Became Known as *The Matheny Manifesto*

In the event you're not familiar with that original letter of mine, here it is. Otherwise, feel free to jump right into chapter 1. (And either way, feel free to use it, adapt it, or borrow from it to shape your own preseason conversation with your team's parents.)

Dear Fellow Parents:

I've always said I would coach only a team of orphans. Why? Because the biggest problem in youth sports is the parents.

But here we are, so it's best I nip this in the bud. If I'm going to do this, I'm asking you to grab the concept that this is going to be ALL about the boys. If anything in this is about you, we need a change of plans.

My main goals are to:

1—teach these boys how to play baseball the right way

2—make a positive impact on them as young men

3—do all this with class

We may not win every game, but we will be the classiest coaches, players, and parents at every game we play. The boys are going to show respect for their teammates, for the opposition, and for the umpires—no matter what.

That being said, you need to know where I stand. I have no hidden agenda, no ulterior motives. My priorities in life will permeate how I coach and what I expect from the boys. My Christian faith guides my life, and while I have never been one to force it down someone's throat, I also think it's cowardly and hypocritical to shy away from what I believe. You parents need to know that when the opportunity presents itself, I will be honest about what I believe. That may make some uncomfortable, but I did that as a player, and I want it out in the open from the beginning that I plan to continue it now.

I believe the biggest role a parent can play is to be a silent source of encouragement. If you ask most boys what they want their parents to do during a game, they'll say, "Nothing." Again, this is ALL about the boys. I know youth-league parents feel they must cheer and shout, "Come on, let's go, you can do it!" but even that just adds more pressure.

I will be putting plenty of pressure on these boys to play the game the right way—with class and respect—and they will put too much pressure on themselves and each other as it is. You need to be the silent, constant source of support.

Let me go on record right now that we will not have good umpiring. The sooner we all understand and accept that, the better off we will be. Pitches that bounce in the dirt will sometimes be called strikes, as will pitches that sail over our heads. Likewise, pitches our guys throw right down the middle will sometimes be called balls.

But at no time will our boys be allowed to show any emotion whatsoever toward the umpire. No shaking their heads, no pouting, no saying anything. That is my job, and I will do it well. I once got paid to handle those guys, and I will let them know when they need to hear something.

Really, I'm doing you a favor you probably don't realize at this point. I have eliminated a lot of work for you. All you have to do is get your son there on time, and enjoy. And all they need to hear from you is that you enjoyed watching them and that you hope they had fun.

I know it's going to be very hard not to coach from the stands and yell encouraging things, but trust me on this: coaching and yelling (even encouraging) work against their development and enjoyment. I'm not saying you can't clap for them when they do well. I'm saying that if you entrust your child to me to coach him, then let me do that job.

That doesn't change the fact that a large part of how much your child improves *is* your responsibility. What makes a difference for kids at this level is how much repetition they get, and that goes for pitching, hitting, and fielding.

You can help out tremendously by playing catch, throwing batting practice, hitting groundballs, or finding an instructor who will do this in your place. The more of this your child can get, the better. The one constant I've found with major leaguers is that someone spent a lot of time with them between games.

I am completely fine with your son getting lessons from whomever you see fit. The only problem I will have is if you or your instructor counters what I'm teaching the team. I won't teach a lot of mechanics at first, but I will teach a mental approach, and I'll expect the boys to comply. If I see your son doing something drastically wrong mechanically, I will talk with you or his instructor and clear it up.

The same will hold true with pitching coaches. We will have a pitching philosophy and will teach pitchers and catchers how to call a game and why we choose the pitches we choose. There'll be no guessing; we'll have reasons for the pitches we throw. A pitching coach will be helpful for the boys to get their arms in shape and be ready to throw when spring arrives. Every boy on this team will be worked as a pitcher. We will not overuse these young arms and will keep a close watch on the number of innings each boy is pitching.

I will be throwing so much info at these boys that they will suffer from overload for a while, but eventually they'll get it. I'm a stickler about the thought process of the game. I'll talk nonstop about situational hitting, situational pitching, and defensive preparation. The question they'll hear most is "What were you thinking?"

What were you thinking when you threw that pitch?

What were you thinking during that at bat?

What were you thinking before the pitch was thrown; what were you anticipating?

I am a firm believer that this game is more mental than physical, and though the mental aspect may be more difficult, it can be learned by ten- and eleven-year-olds.

If it sounds like I'm going to be demanding, you're exactly right. I'm definitely going to demand their attention, and I'm going to require effort.

Attitude, concentration, and effort are three things they can control. If they give me those three things every time they show up, they will have a great experience.

It works best for all of us if you would plan on turning your kid over to me and the assistant coaches when you drop him off and plan on his being mine for the two hours or so that we have scheduled for a game or practice. I want him to take responsibility for his own water, not have you running to the concession stand or standing behind the dugout asking if he's thirsty or hungry or hot—and I'd appreciate if you would share this information with other guests, like grandparents.

If there is an injury, obviously we'll call you, but otherwise let's pretend he's at work for a short time and that you've been granted the privilege of watching. I want them at games early so we can stretch and loosen up, and I will have a meeting with just the boys after the game. After that they are all yours again.

As I'm writing this I realize I sound like a kids' baseball Nazi, but I really believe this will make things easier for everyone involved.

(And as I was reading this, believe me, I knew it was coming across even stronger than when I had been writing it. In my peripheral vision I could tell mouths were hanging open. I began seriously considering what else I could do with my spare time that summer.)

Now let me be clear about family priorities. I'm a firm believer that the family is the most important institution in the lives of these guys. Family events are much more important than the sports events. I just ask that you show consideration to the rest of the team and let the team manager and me know when your son will miss practice or a game, and let us know as soon as possible. There will be times when *I* have to miss for family reasons or other commitments.

So, if your son misses a game or a practice, it's not the end of the world, but out of respect for the kids that *have* made it, he may be asked to run, have his playing time altered a bit, or even be moved down in the batting order.

Along with where he hits in the lineup and his amount of playing time, which position a kid plays is one of the most complained-about issues. I need you to know that I am trying to develop each boy individually, and I will give him a chance to learn and play any position he is interested in. I will have each tell me his favorite position and what other position he would like to learn about.

I believe this team will eventually be competitive. When we get to where we are focusing on winning, like in a tournament for example, we are going to put the boys in the positions that will give us the best opportunity. Meanwhile, as the season progresses, there's a chance your son may be playing a position he doesn't like. That's when I most need your support about his role on the team.

I know times have changed, but one of the greatest lessons my father taught me was that my coach was always right—even when he was wrong. That principle is a great life lesson about how things really work. Our culture has lost respect for authority, because kids hear their parents complain about teachers and coaches. That said, I'm determined to exhibit enough humility to come to your son and apologize if I've treated him wrong. Meanwhile, give me the benefit of the doubt that I have his best interest in mind, even if you're convinced I'm wrong.

I need you to know that we are most likely going to lose many games this year. The main reason is that we need to find out how we measure up against the local talent pool, and the only way to know that is to play against some of the best teams. I'm convinced that if the boys put their work in at home and give me their best effort, we'll be able to play with just about any team. Time will tell.

I also believe there is enough local talent that we will not have to do a large amount of travel, if any. That may be disappointing for those who play only baseball and look forward to the out-of-town experiences. But I also know this will be a relief for parents who have traveled throughout the US and Canada for hockey and soccer looking for better competition. In my experience, we have traveled all over the Midwest and have found just as good competition right in our backyard. If this season goes well, we will entertain the idea of travel in the future.

The boys will be required to show up ready to play every time they come to the field. That means shirts tucked in, hats on straight, and no pants drooping to their knees.

There is never an excuse for lack of hustle on a baseball field. From the first step outside the dugout they will hustle. They will quickly jog to their positions, to the plate, and back to the bench after an out. We will run out every hit harder than any team we play, and we will learn to always back up our teammates. Every single play, every player will be required to move to a spot. Players who don't hustle and run out balls will not play. The boys will catch onto this quickly.

Baseball becomes very boring when players are not thinking about the next play and what they could possibly do to help the team. Players on the bench will not be messing around. I will constantly talk with them about situations and what they would do in a specific position or if they were the batter. There is as much to learn on the bench as there is on the field.

All this will take time for the boys to conform to. They are kids, and I am not trying to take away from that, but I believe they can bear down and concentrate during games and practices.

I know this works because it was how I was taught the game and how our parents acted in the stands. We started our Little League team when I was ten years old in a small suburb of Columbus, Ohio. We had a very disciplined coach who expected the same from us. We committed eight summers to this man, and we were rewarded for our efforts. I went to Michigan, one teammate went to Miami of Florida, one to Ohio State, two to North Carolina, one to Central Florida, two to Kent State, and most of the others played smaller Division 1 or Division 2 baseball. Five of us went on to play professionally—not a bad showing from a small-town team.

I'm not guaranteeing this is what's going to happen to our boys, but I want you to see that this system works. I know that by now you're asking if this is what you want to get yourself into, and I understand that for some it may not be the right fit. But I also think there's a great opportunity here for these boys to grow together and learn lessons that will last far beyond their baseball experience.

Let me know as soon as possible whether or not this is a commitment that you and your son want to make.

Thanks,
Mike

Section One

Before the Season Begins

1

Defining Success

Your Goals and Your Message

You might come at this role in one of a number of different ways. Maybe you've coached before. Maybe you haven't. Maybe you really wanted this job and volunteered for it. Maybe you didn't and were cajoled into it.

Regardless, you're now the coach. Willingly, reluctantly, or otherwise, you want to give it all you have. I'm already on record that you don't want to take *yourself* too seriously. In other words, don't affect some persona of a big shot to whom winning "isn't everything; it's the only thing." I know, that made sense for the legendary Vince Lombardi of Green Bay Packers fame. But again, and I'll be playing this tune throughout, the kids you coach are not professional athletes with virtually everything in their lives riding on their team's win-loss record.

Frankly, I've seen too many youth-league coaches who try to dress and act the part of the give-no-quarter leader. They strut, they scowl, they yell. In the end, they do the opposite of what I recommend.

Now that's not to say you shouldn't take your *role* seriously. Whether you intend it or not, as soon as a kid joins your team, you become a role model.

The question is, what are you going to model?

I can imagine what you're feeling if you're brand-new to this. You're wondering, even before you have any idea who will be on your team: Where do I start? What do I do first?

Well, if you agree with me that molding kids into the best adults they can become is more important than turning them into a championship team or all-star baseball players, run every decision you make through that grid. What's best for each future man? That should weigh on every decision you make about your team from day one.

Of course, you want to communicate your goals and your message in concert with, not independent of, your team's parents. But as my manifesto letter implies, you'll find that's a delicate dance that requires firm boundaries and clear expectations (see chapter 3).

My goal is to give you everything you need to be the most effective coach you can be. That means I want to make sure this book is full of drills and exercises and strategy tips, including videos from many trusted experts and me. Start with my introductory video at the QR code here, and I'll point to the rest of the videos throughout so you'll know what to teach and how to teach it, trying to be sure the nuts-and-bolts side of baseball is thoroughly covered. (At any point, feel free to jump to chapters 7 and 8 for explanations of the various drills.)

Intro

But since I am also on record that the character side of the equation is by far the most important, I want to give you an idea of how I have always tried to set the tone for my teams—whether ten-year-olds or big leaguers. While I did emphasize winning with big leaguers—it's what they're paid to do, after all—I urge you to emphasize fun, learning, and character. If you get those right, winning will eventually follow.

Once you've established who your players will be—and how you go about this will vary depending on your local league procedures (tryouts or randomly assigned kids)—your first address to the team becomes the foundation of everything you're trying to accomplish. To be clear, this would be a meeting of just you (and any assistant coaches you can recruit) and the players, not with their parents, and it would take place even before your first practice. So, have your plan and bring your notes, but whatever you do, don't read your speech. Maintain eye contact with the team as much as possible, peeking at your notes only as needed.

Just be sure, wherever and whenever you present this, to read the room. If there's one thing I've learned as a coach and manager, it's that individual players are more sensitive than they've ever been—and some much more so than others. Being old-school, I'm from a generation where players didn't generally express our feelings. We might say a few things privately to each other or vent to our families in the privacy of our own homes. But we never wanted to show weakness or vulnerability in front of our manager and coaches. If we got called out, reamed out, even shown up, we sucked it up, licked our own wounds, and stayed at the task.

That's not so common anymore. With an epidemic of anxiety sweeping the younger generations, you can expect to find fragile, sometimes broken, kids at every level. Sometimes it's hard to resist the temptation to tell them to grow up and get over it, but there's little upside to that.

This doesn't mean you should coddle players. Just be aware that they may have issues, difficult home lives, estranged parents, and all kinds of other stress factors at play. That makes it all the more important that you model and teach the life skills that will help kids cope, turning them into adults who can both live and pass along those values.

With that in mind, let me share with you a few life lessons I've learned along the way. I call these Competitive EDGES, and that second word serves as an acrostic for five distinct points. I have been fortunate to meet and even in some cases play with some of the greatest baseball players in history. I've found that these men display character qualities that helped them beat overwhelming odds and achieve their dreams. While making the major leagues should be a *very* low priority for your team, these same qualities apply to every relationship they enjoy. So while the examples I use may be from those ones-in-a-million who did become big leaguers, they can apply to any endeavor.

Five qualities you can model and teach your players serve as Competitive EDGES everyone needs to succeed—not just in sports, but also in life.

Competitive EDGES: Education

I'm not talking about the formal education that comes through institutions of higher learning—as important as that is. I'm talking about street smarts, life smarts—the art of staying curious and seeking always to learn something new. Making such a pursuit a lifestyle habit can result in a gift that keeps on giving for a lifetime.

I have attended many coaching seminars at various competition levels, and I always learn something. The key is to approach these with the right mindset, never assuming you already know it all. Watch for clinics and conferences in your area, even if they are intended for high school athletes or older. You might be surprised at how much of what you learn can be applied to your young players.

Don't be afraid to offer parents your help in emphasizing the importance of the boys' schoolwork. I will never forget, as a ten-year-old baseball player, having my coach tell me he was going to collect my report card every six weeks and that he would pay close attention to the teachers' remarks about my effort and attitude in their classes. That extra bit of accountability really motivated me.

Later, when I coached young boys, I found that their parents appreciated my emphasis on academic excellence. Obviously, the parents should play the lead role here, but most love having outside support.

Along with this offer to be an extra eye for the parents comes the responsibility to follow up. Many parents allowed me full rein to manipulate playing time or to otherwise motivate the boys if they were not doing their part in the classroom.

I believe I would not have had the playing career I had without having taken my academics seriously in grade school, which led to the same in high school and to the University of Michigan. I doubt I would have managed in the major leagues without earning my degree. That's becoming more important all the time, as teams search for leaders with both talent and the ability to adapt and change with the ever-evolving game.

One of the greatest coaches I was ever exposed to was George Kissell, a legend in the St. Louis Cardinals organization. I had heard about Kissell before I ever wore a Cardinal jersey, because though he never played more than minor-league ball, he became a minor-league manager, a big-league coach, and so respected a teacher of the game that he became known as "The Professor." Some considered him a Mr. Miyagi type when it came to teaching the intricacies of baseball.

Kissell was signed as an infielder by Branch Rickey in 1940 and worked within the Cardinals organization for nearly seventy years. He mentored such major-league managers as Sparky Anderson, Joe Torre, and Tony La Russa.

Late in his life he served the Cardinals as field coordinator of system-wide instruction, then senior field coordinator. The Cardinals still annually honor a minor-league coach with the George Kissell Award. Former Cardinal manager Whitey Herzog once said, "George Kissell is the only man I know who can talk for fifteen minutes about a groundball."

Though I'd long been aware of his reputation, I first met George in 2000 when I was invited to spring training as a potential backup catcher for the Cardinals after a six-year career. I was on the bench watching a game when Kissell, already nearly eighty, sat next to me and began rapid-firing questions at me about baseball philosophy, strategy, and other personnel who had been invited to camp.

Uh-oh, I thought, my palms getting sweaty as I stumbled through this pop-quiz test of my baseball IQ. I desperately wanted to pass if it would help me make the team. But I noticed something in George's eyes that has stuck with me ever since. I could see in how he asked questions and responded to my answers that he was not judging me. Even at that stage of his life and career, he was actually trying to learn something from my answers. I could hardly believe it—*him* learning from *me*? This man who had coached some of the greatest players in history and mentored some of the greatest managers had enough humility to think he could learn something from some scrub who had just been released twice and was trying to hang on.

I learned that day that some people never lose their desire to be educated. That celebrated senior citizen proved more curious than most of the players in uniform that day. A lifelong student of the game felt he had more to learn. He reminded me of John Wooden, who was known to say, "It's what you learn after you know it all that counts."

A Challenge

Study the greatest amateur coaches of all time and you'll find they have a few things in common. If they're the greatest, they have obviously been successful, but a healthy win-loss record has never been their primary goal. This is similar to great leaders in any profession. Investing in your people helps them thrive in the workplace. The winningest coaches have done the same thing with the kids they've been honored to lead.

In his book, *The Ideal Team Player,* Patrick Lencioni summarizes the most crucial qualities as being humble, hungry, and smart. It takes humility to admit that we don't have it all figured out and that we could still learn from the least likely of teachers. Our hunger for wisdom will be evident by what we read, who we listen to, and how active we are in searching out mentors. The smart component really comes down to a willingness to put the lessons into action.

This concept of obtaining a competitive edge through Education becomes a habit derived from a mindset of growth. Carol Dweck, a Stanford professor, wrote a great book titled *Mindset,* which divides people into those with a *fixed* mindset and those with a *growth* mindset. Those with the latter simply see life differently.

Not all of us will become teaching legends like George Kissell, but all of us have the opportunity to grow in the areas of life important to us. I like to ask people what the most important things are in their lives—hoping the answers do not actually include tangible "things," but rather relationships and people. I often ask myself whether I'm actively, intentionally trying to grow those important relationships? If not, they must not be that important after all.

Greatness comes with lifelong learning—Education.

Competitive EDGES: Discipline

You'll hear many different definitions of *Discipline,* but I like to think of it as a quality that answers the question of whether I can trust you.

Another way of thinking about Discipline is to simplify it to "doing the right thing." Put that together with my question and you get, "Can I trust you to do the right thing?"

So simple, yet so profound. Often, we know the next right thing to do, but do we do it? The bigger question comes when we try to decipher between good things and the right thing. A former coach of mine, Chris Bando, says, "Good things become bad things when they keep you from the best things."

I was reminded of this as a manager when I once committed to spend as much time with my family as possible during a ten-game home stand. Man, did I mess that up. Despite my lofty plans, I failed to proactively prioritize my time, and it flew by. And it wasn't that I was doing bad things. I was doing good things! I spent the week and a half raising funds for various charities and trying to help people out. But that commitment to my family fell by the wayside. My intentions were noble, but I failed to follow through. We might have gone camping, hunting, enjoyed an amusement park, just played together, or gone out for ice cream.

I messed up my opportunity to honor the most important people in my life. Talk about good things becoming bad things when they keep you from the best things . . .

How does this relate to coaching? I'm sure that like me, you want to be successful, but we can all get distracted by things that seem important. Without a plan to keep first things first, we set ourselves up for failure. Many coaches believe that the more time they spend with their sport, the better they are going to be. Sadly,

I've seen legendary coaches spend so much time in the clubhouse that, long after the game is over, they've lost their families.

Fortunately, this is changing. The best professional coaches go home when the game and their media responsibilities are over, and they insist that their assistants do the same. I know some big-league managers who don't allow their coaches and players to show up until later in the day, so they can spend time with their families. Such coaches understand the value of a proper balance between their careers and their families, and somehow they become more effective at home and at work.

Survival of the Fittest

I learned a lot about working with young kids from my time in professional baseball, both as a player coming up and later as a manager. Let me explain. In pro ball there's a weeding—or vetting—course called the minor leagues. I have always loved how one has to fight his way through the ranks to reach the highest level. Some other sports miss the lessons that can be learned through the hardships of a minor-league system. As a minor leaguer in the early 1990s, my pretax monthly income was about $800, and I had to figure out living arrangements and how to eat on what was left. We played because we loved the game and dreamt of playing in the majors.

Later, as a manager, every spring I made sure to speak to the minor-league players who were in major-league camp for the first time. I tried to clearly lay out the expectations. I told them, "Be on time. Work hard. Ask good questions. Get here early, stay as late as you can, and soak in as much as possible. Most of you are here for the learning experience and quite honestly have little chance of making our club, but the time you spend here now can help you get back here someday and stay."

I then warned them of the inevitable challenges. "Your friends and family will be excited for you, but be careful that you don't confuse spring training with spring break. You are going to feel tempted to act differently because more people will know your name, and they will treat you like you're somebody. You're going to be tempted to start acting like a big leaguer, because you're rubbing elbows with them every day. You might even think you should be heading to the golf course when you actually have more work to do. You may be tempted to hit the nightlife a little harder than normal. But you have about six weeks to make a good impression here, to learn the culture and the expectations of a major-league team and show off your skills. Make the most of it, boys, and don't leave here with any regrets."

After I give this caution, the guys are clearly excited about the opportunity, and I see in their eyes and even sometimes hear them say, "Not me. I'm here to work." I believe them and believe they believe themselves. But soon it gets hard. The first couple of days, the rookies bust their butts, get to the stadium early, stay late, and outwork everyone. But by about day three, some of the veterans will give them grief about how hard they're working, and peer pressure starts to set in. They tease the rookies, warning them not to show up the veterans, but in reality that's just a mind game to keep someone from taking their jobs. Not long later, one of the young guys shows up late. Soon we get word that a certain room at the team hotel is making too much noise until the wee hours of the night. Sometimes the local police call to let us know there is "an issue."

Now, please know that these are good kids. They really are, and they're just having fun, kids being kids and enjoying a rare opportunity. I get it. But I also know from experience that if they can't handle the distractions in spring training, there's little chance they can handle what comes when the big lights turn on. Quite simply, we can't trust them to do the right thing—yet. They're undisciplined.

Let me be clear, we're not looking for choirboys or robots. Our guys need to be able to breathe and have fun. What top-tier players figure out, though, is how to prioritize what is right versus what will keep them from the kind of career they dream of. Today's players truly are more disciplined than ever before. They realize how small the window of opportunity is and they understand their earning potential if they can exhibit the Discipline needed.

What would you be willing to do for the next six weeks if it would help you reach your dream? What would you be willing to stay away from for the next six weeks, if you knew it would cost you that dream? That's the definition of Discipline—a competitive edge that pays dividends over time.

Competitive EDGES: Grit

I don't know of a more flattering description of a baseball player than that he's gritty.

Every occupation has a certain amount of grind. You know what I mean, because that's likely true of your profession, whatever it is. The real test for baseball players is not so much the physical demands of a big-league season—though that can be brutal—but the mental endurance. I don't know of many jobs where you must be "on" for as many days as professional baseball players are in a nine-month period.

Don't get me wrong. No one wants to hear well-paid professionals whine about how tough their lives are. I'm fully aware of the advantages of playing a game for a living as opposed to living in the real world. But many players can't handle the high level of scrutiny under the media and public microscope, and it shortens their careers. That's why they need Grit.

The coaches and managers I admire most have a level of perseverance that carries through an entire clubhouse. I always considered it the ultimate compliment if my teams developed a reputation for fighting and pushing through tough stretches of the season. One national writer wrote about one of my teams, "They are like a horror movie villain. They just won't go away." I swelled with pride when I read that to the guys before the playoffs that season. They needed to know how they were viewed and to be proud of their reputation.

Believe it or not, the need for toughness can be downright scary to some of the players in a big-league clubhouse. Some managers and coaches try to create it through fear and intimidation. That style of coaching may have worked in a previous generation, but the majority of today's athletes simply shut down under it.

But please hear what I am also *not* saying. Leadership must not appear docile either. Gritty, strong, servant leadership is magnetic.

I like how Jim Collins talks about the level-five leader in his classic *Good to Great.* Collins explains how a gritty leader takes every opportunity to absorb criticism. He's the first to stand in front of the mirror and say, "This is on me, and I will own it!"

That type of a leader is also the first to deflect the praise that inevitably comes to the company of a strong leader. The leader with Grit will walk to the window and say, "Look at my people and what they have accomplished!"

For that type of leader, I will run through a brick wall. I know he has my back, and I also know he is praising me for things he had a hand in too.

Obviously a level of physical toughness comes with Grit—whether that means playing with an injury or while ill, and not making excuses. This requires something deep within a person's character, and you have to be very careful how you manage this with youngsters, especially in that 6–8 year-old range. Clearly, I wouldn't recommend badgering a kid to play when he's hurt or sick. But you'll know when a player is just complaining of being tired or suffers from minor aches and pains.

Much like perseverance in adversity, Grit usually manifests in the fires of hardship. I enjoy helping players test the limits of their pain tolerance and seeing how proud they are when they do their job in spite of it all. But again, the younger your players are, the more cautious you must be about pushing them to their limits.

I deeply respect the men and women in our armed forces. I've had the pleasure of knowing and learning from some of our special ops personnel, and I am humbled by their true Grit. With everything on the line, these warriors find another gear when things get really tough. And talk about humility. Don't waste your time trying to praise these brave people. Most of them simply have a deeper *Why* than most.

Nineteenth-century philosopher Friedrich Nietzsche said, "He who has a *why* to live for can bear almost any *how*." I'll get back to *Why* when we get to the S in EDGES, but for now suffice it to say that the toughest people in any industry, including baseball, find ways to scratch out a competitive advantage when the odds are stacked against them.

People with Grit stand out from the crowd.

Competitive EDGES: Enthusiasm

One of the key characteristics of a coach who leaves a positive impact is Enthusiasm.

Enthusiasm is displayed with energy and optimism. The late

General Colin Powell said, "Perpetual optimism is a force multiplier."

I believe the opposite of this statement is also true: perpetual pessimism is a force divider. The strongest ally of pessimism is complaining, and it's amazing how quickly this creeps into a team and the complaining becomes gossip. This can happen at the youth-league level, too, so you'll want to be vigilant against it. Something I tried to convince players of in my big-league clubhouses as early as spring training is that the team culture is an extension of the way people treat each other.

There's nothing wrong with your trying to engender a culture of selflessly serving others in the dugout or on the field. Encourage the guys to stay far from backstabbing and force themselves to search for ways to challenge and encourage each other.

Everybody knows the Golden Rule: Treat people the way you want to be treated. Too many people, however, never know what it feels like to be treated like they want to be treated. But if they can be taught to serve the people around them, with no thought of getting anything in return, eventually contagious generosity will make its way back to them.

It starts with you, coach, modeling doing the right thing.

Let Kids Dream

To keep your team enthusiastic, be careful not to squelch their imaginations. Do you remember when we were kids how we used to pretend that we were cowboys, astronauts, superheroes, or big-league baseball players? These days those dreams might also include rapper, reality TV star, or business tycoon . . . how times have changed! When you're a kid you have complete freedom to dream. You have the ability to believe that anything is possible, because the world has yet to prevent you from believing otherwise. It's such a gift. I happen to believe that we ultimately create our own destiny based on the choices we make every day. Just think about it. Every day we can choose to wake up early or sleep in. We can choose to work hard or just get by. We can choose to put good things in our minds, or to fill ourselves with useless junk. We can choose to eat right, or to eat fast food. I think you get the point. Our choices are within our control.

If we make the same choices (good or bad) consistently, those choices will become habits. I've heard it said that it takes twenty-one days to form a habit. I'm not really sure about that exact number but it seems like a reasonable estimate. The good news is that habits are pure momentum in our lives. They will take us to the top or straight into the ground if not managed properly. It's our job to use them wisely to create the future that we desire.

I think some people are scared to encourage their kids to dream because they fear it will create disappointment later when life doesn't turn out the way they hoped. My thought is this: Encourage your kids to use their imaginations. Listen to them without judgment. The encouragement and belief you provide will energize them. Your job is to then focus that energy toward good choices. Explain that they need to make the right choices every day to reach their goals. Those simple everyday choices will develop good habits. Those good habits will ultimately cause them to achieve their dreams. By the way, it works the same for big people. I dare you to give it a try.

Two Ears and One Mouth

I've heard it said that it's no coincidence that God gave us two ears and just one mouth. Make a pact with your assistant coaches to go an entire day without complaining, and then see if you can do a week, then a month, then the whole season.

The best thing about positivity is that it is always an option. At both the professional and amateur levels, it is nonnegotiable. Regardless of where you see yourself on the spectrum of coaching experience or ability, commit to optimism. Enthusiasm alone can separate you from the crowd.

Life doesn't always deal us a fair hand and can at times feel overwhelming. While I have mostly lived a charmed life and have been privileged to reap many benefits from it, like anyone else I've had my share of tough blows. I've made decisions I regret, suffered consequences I deserved, and have also been treated unfairly, unjustly, unkindly. In the throes of such experiences, we are still asked to coach, to live out our marriage vows, to be model parents. At times like that, high levels of energy and Enthusiasm can be a tough ask.

So what do we do? Enthusiastically, proactively encourage someone else.

You want to know how to recognize someone who needs encouragement? Check to see if they have a pulse. Even the most talented baseball players on the planet are often starved for some form of encouragement. We *all* need it, more often than we care to admit.

Combine Enthusiasm, energy, and encouragement, and you create what I like to call the E-Flywheel. Look up the definition of a *flywheel* and you'll find a technical description of a heavy revolving wheel designed to increase a machine's momentum and provide more stability or a reserve of power. So a flywheel self-perpetuates and even multiplies. That's how I see Enthusiasm contributing to what we're after as coaches.

Encouragement draws others into the cycle and helps create an atmosphere they want to be a part of—a culture fertile for growth and improvement. Somehow the giving we do to help others seems to return to us. As a person of faith, I like to call this phenomenon the "miracle of reciprocity." But even people who don't share my beliefs imagine that somehow the universe and karma are at play here. I'm convinced that when we choose to invest in others by encouraging them with both energy and Enthusiasm, a divine miracle occurs: by focusing on something bigger than ourselves, we are freed from the stress and anxiety of our own circumstances.

Competitive EDGES: Selflessness

A basic truth: whether you're coaching a youth-league team or a big-league franchise, talent sets your players apart. And talent is important. However, I'll take attitude over talent any day, all day, every day. I've played with some of the greatest players the game has ever seen, and some—fortunately only a few—were toxic to the team. Even if they made millions of dollars and produced numbers that should have guaranteed them the Hall of Fame, most of their teammates have bad tastes in their mouths when recalling playing with them.

How sad is that?

Now, give me a superstar talent who also evidences these Competitive EDGES, who blends the traits they're born with and the ones they can control, and you have the ultimate teammate.

But of the EDGES, why is Selflessness such a big deal?

The pull of selfishness is strong. Something deep inside all of us tells us we need to take care of ourselves or else nobody will. Additionally, each day we're targeted by billions of advertising dollars trying to convince us to get all we can, for as long as we can, so we can go sit on our can. (Thanks to my longtime friend and mentor Mike Hansen for that gem.)

But when we're somehow able to battle these forces, everything changes. The rewards of an "others-first" mindset are huge, but it is difficult to develop and even harder to maintain.

In the big leagues, Selflessness seems impossible, because players have multiple people in their ears trying to convince them that the only things that matter are their personal statistics, the numbers that determine how much they can make. Those voices aren't wrong—at least in theory.

But too few of those voices understand the miracle of reciprocity—something I've witnessed firsthand. I've seen veteran players choose to help the young, highly touted rookies pressing to take their jobs, rather than sabotage them. In my experience, the true greats push past the painful reality that their careers are coming to an end and share the secrets they've learned along the trail, determined to do the right thing for the newcomer and for the team.

That kind of a team concept is hard to teach, and many will never accept it. But when you see your best players live it out, it's often because someone else once did that for them. And even better, a true phenomenon happens when we give in this way. The more these players give of themselves to others, the better their own game becomes in the twilight of their careers.

Now, this won't play out the same on your youth-league team, because few, say, twelve-year-olds are mature enough to counsel or model for kids just a year or two younger than they are. But surely you can see what a priceless character quality Selflessness can be for every player. While they won't likely be risking their playing time to some upstart, imagine what kind of men they can become as they learn to put others above themselves. As they get into junior and senior high school, they can become extremely valuable teammates, especially to the younger players.

The absolute highest compliment a player can be given is that he is a great teammate—and I'll cover later what goes into gaining that reputation. And while all five of these Competitive EDGES help define a great teammate, in many ways Selflessness stands alone. When a player stands in front of a TV camera with millions of fans watching and takes full responsibility when things go wrong, all the while directing praise toward his teammates when the world wants to elevate him, his street cred in the clubhouse goes through the roof. It takes outrageous Grit and courage to exude that level of Selflessness, and those are the kinds of players you win with. Especially when the truth is that often someone else did *not* do their job properly.

When individuals decide to exercise Selflessness, things happen. If it's true that anxiety is the unspoken villain among all ages today—and I believe it is—Selflessness has to be one of the antidotes. Get kids motivated to turn their attention to someone else, and watch them flourish.

When members of the US elite military special forces are asked why they do what they do, they usually acknowledge their commitment to the welfare of their teammates as their driving force. People will often do things for others that they would not do for themselves. Their *Why* is not about them. Their *Why* is about everyone around them, and they know their comrades care just as much for them.

So I challenge you to try to adopt these EDGES in your life and to model them with the intent to instill in your young team members values that would nudge them to selflessly serve others. Then, regardless of their future in baseball, any relationship in their lives will be better and stronger. Imagine accomplishing that.

I know all this selfless-serving stuff can come off a little soft, but ask yourself who is most widely credited with being the greatest leader of all time. I will not force my faith down anyone's throat, but I will also not turn a blind eye to the fact that leadership is measured by followership. Jesus Christ has more followers than anyone—more than two thousand years since he walked the earth. And how did he lead? He said, "I came to serve, not to be served."

True leadership is Selfless, servant leadership.

Selflessness reduces anxiety, frees athletes to be better, multiplies effort by making teammates better, and ironically increases the odds of winning. I've also found that a selfless player is usually the most respected and liked player on any team—in short, a great teammate.

One of the bravest men to ever wear a major-league uniform was the great Jackie Robinson, who said this: "A life is unimportant outside of the impact it has on other lives."

Imagine the kind of a teammate he must have been.

2

What a Great Teammate Looks Like

Notice my chapter title here has nothing to do with being a great player. Even some great MLB players never enjoyed the title of "great teammate," and I would guess most of them eventually left the game with deep regret. They might still be rightly proud of their individual accomplishments, but they have to grieve the memory of loneliness—of achieving fame and accolades without the love, support, and camaraderie of doing something special with other members of the team.

Being known as a great teammate should be the goal of each of your players.

If I'm right that the foundational characteristic of someone with the five Competitive EDGES is Selflessness, it's important to understand the best definition of true humility. This is not original to me, but it goes like this: "Humility is not thinking less of yourself, but thinking of yourself less." That has been attributed to C. S. Lewis in *Mere Christianity*, but in truth it originated with Rick Warren in his classic *The Purpose Driven Life*.

The reason it may have long been miscredited to Lewis is that he wrote something similar and every bit as poignant in 1952:

> Do not imagine that if you meet a really humble man he will be what most people call "humble" nowadays: he will not be a sort of greasy, smarmy person, who is always telling you that, of course, he is nobody. Probably all you will think about him is that he seemed a cheerful, intelligent chap who took a real interest in what you said to him. If you do dislike him it will be because you feel a little envious of anyone who seems to enjoy life so easily. He will not be thinking about humility: he will not be thinking about himself at all.
>
> If anyone would like to acquire humility, I can, I think, tell him the first step. The first step is to realize that one is proud. And a biggish step, too. At least, nothing whatever can be done before it. If you think you are not conceited, it means you are very conceited indeed.*

Selflessness is rare and powerful, and creating a culture infused with it will make practice a pleasure to show up to every day. You may find you have kids on your team who prefer their teammates more than their own families. That's a sad commentary on modern life, but it's also a reality. The true family feel of a team of selfless players increases the chances for personal growth. Selfish players will retreat to an island of solitude, a tough place from which to succeed.

Also, as I've tried to point out, selflessness tends to breed selflessness. If everyone's into it, from you as the head coach to your assistants to your players and—who knows?—even the parents, everyone will be more willing to help *you* by offering their time, support, and gratitude. That's something any new coach will appreciate.

---

* C. S. Lewis, *Mere Christianity* (New York: HarperOne, 2001), 128.

Playing Kids at the Proper Level

Here is another sticky issue you may run into. We all remember the kid we grew up with who was a man-child at the age of twelve and dominated every sport he played. Several years before I was born, a twelve-year-old who was 6'1" and 185 pounds played in the 1962 Little League World Series. No surprise, his team won.

But those man-child kids almost always find that as they get older, the talent gap shrinks until, one day, they simply blend in with the rest of the kids their age. They've never had to learn how to handle adversity or face competition that forced them to improve. I'm so grateful that I was a late bloomer and one of the smallest kids in my class, because it made me work harder just to survive—let alone to achieve.

The best thing you can do as a coach if you find yourself blessed with one of these wonders of nature? Consider the fact that he may not be the best teammate for your other players, but even more importantly, search for the proper competition level for him—for *his* sake. I know it's tough to let go of a kid who could win a lot of ball games for you, but this is all about the kids, right? Not about the trophies. What's best for him?

We want our kids to have fun and play with their friends, but we also want to see them become successful. Let a kid like that dominate at a lower level, and he learns what? Nothing. His peers eventually catch up with him, and he flames out or loses interest. I've seen this even at the big-league level where certain guys who never struggled before are finally facing the best players in the world, and they don't know how to handle it. They've never learned how to compete.

What kind of a man are we raising when that happens? Make a tough decision as a coach and tell his parents that their child should play on another team at a higher level.

Seize the Day

Another hallmark of a player who becomes a valued teammate is that he has learned to seize the day, the message of the 1989 movie *Dead Poets Society,* where the late Robin Williams, playing boarding school teacher John Keating, takes his students to the school's trophy case. There, among the dusty old pictures of former student athletes, the boys in his class see the faded memories of kids just like themselves who thought they would go on to conquer the world. Williams/Keating tells his class that those kids in the old black-and-white photographs are "not that different from you, are they?" He points out that they have similar haircuts, and that they're full of hormones and likely feeling invincible, "just like you." The teacher opines that back in that day, those boys considered the world their oyster and that they were destined for great things, their eyes full of hope. He asks if those boys waited until it was too late to accomplish even an iota of what they were capable. Now long dead, he says, their legacy lives on: *Carpe diem.* Seize the day. "Make your lives extraordinary."

I love that term because it can cause us to speed up and slow down at the same time. Speed to make the most of each day, and slow to make sure we keep our priorities in order. Too often we don't see the urgency of what is right in front of us. We neglect to take advantage of today's opportunity and the privilege we have to make an impact on the people entrusted to us. Maybe we get distracted by some long-term vision and forget to make the most of the present.

It's been said that yesterday is a canceled check and tomorrow is a promissory note, so the only cash we have to spend is today. Spend it wisely. There's always something to strive for, to learn, to accomplish—today. That's why we want to imbue character into our players. So they'll make the most of every day, every practice, every interaction, every relationship. That's sure to make them better teammates.

Carpe diem.

The Movie *42*

It's hard to believe that at the time of this writing, *42,* the Jackie Robinson movie, is already more than ten years old. If you haven't seen it, you must. I urge you to find it on a streaming service and show it to your team members. It is rated PG-13, so you'll have to clear it with your players' parents, but check it out and show those you—and they—believe are old enough to appreciate it.

The movie does a great job bringing to life the story of Jackie Robinson and his heroic courage in breaking baseball's shameful color barrier. Jackie was the hope for everyone who believed in a better way. No doubt he knew how important it was for him to do what he did, but I wonder if he realized how monumental a difference he made in our world.

Neither you nor I will likely change the world like No. 42 did, but don't sell short the impact you can have on making better teammates of the young men who look up to you every day.

The Value of Adversity

In my personal as well as professional life, I have without a doubt learned more from my failures—and the struggles that came from them—than I ever have from my successes. Yes, the highs can be high and even profitable, but it's uncanny how much growth and, yes, wisdom can come from failure.

Baseball is a game chock-full of failure, but I seemed to suffer more of it than most at certain times during my career. Though in the end I could look back on a long and mostly satisfying thirteen-year career—way longer than the average tenure of just over five and a half years—I was released twice. I started as the backup catcher for the Milwaukee Brewers for two years, then became the starter for the next three. I assumed I was in good stead with the team and would have been happy to remain a Brewer for as long as I wore a uniform. So imagine my surprise—to put it mildly—when the Brewers informed me, about two weeks before Christmas of 1999, that they were going to let me go.

By that point in the offseason, most of the free agent jobs had been taken, so my agent and I were completely unprepared when the ball club told us they couldn't even trade me. In a panic, we conducted a mad search for any team that might need catching help. I ended up signing with Toronto as a backup catcher unlikely to see much playing time. How quickly things changed from big-league starter to benchwarmer.

As expected, I didn't play much and found myself released yet again. The handwriting on the wall seemed pretty clear: my major-league career was coming to an abrupt end. Kristin and I had just had our fourth child, and the reality of life after baseball was smacking me squarely in the face. Do I continue to chase a job in baseball or venture into the real world and try to put my college degree to use?

Fortunately, St. Louis Cardinals manager Tony La Russa offered me a nonroster invitation to spring training, with no guarantees of making the team or even a role on a minor-league affiliate. Thank goodness, Tony and pitching coach Dave Duncan saw something that the rest of baseball didn't, and they gave me a spot on the team. Eight months later, I was awarded the first of my four Gold Glove Awards, and a career was resurrected.

Another lesson born of that near failure: I learned later that the reason I got the opportunity with St. Louis was that one of my Toronto Blue Jays teammates, Pat Hentgen, signed with the Cardinals in the 1999 offseason. Apparently he told the Cardinals that a backup catcher in Toronto blocked every ball in the dirt in the bullpen and studied the opposition film like no other receiver he'd ever had. That endorsement from a former Cy Young Award winner led to over twenty years in the major leagues as a player and manager.

I could have pouted and just gone through the motions as a backup catcher, but committing to doing the right thing all the time paid huge dividends. You simply never know who is watching.

Another Failure That Led to Success

As I was finishing my playing career, I studied to get my real estate license. I loved baseball, but by now Kristin and I had five young kids and an expensive lifestyle that included private schools, sports, travel, and dreams of making an impact on the world. Knowing that not many players played into their late thirties, I knew I would need to continue to generate income—and I also wanted to contribute meaningfully to society. I had no idea that I would become a big-league manager, so real estate especially intrigued me.

In the early 2000s, while I was still playing, I had invested in a few deals that went really well. Little did I know that the real estate boom at that time would prove to be a false indicator of future success. I had done my homework and told myself I had a knack for the business, but the truth is, I could have thrown a dart at all the real estate possibilities at that time and have had a good chance of hitting something that would work out well.

I partnered with a couple of other investors and did so well that we decided to roll our proceeds into larger projects. Things seemed to be rolling along well until the fall of 2008, when the market took a severe hit, some of our tenants pulled out, and the economy tanked. Things got so bad that the entire mess was left in my incapable hands. For three years, while I was coaching a group of young baseball players, I fought with banks for our financial future and feared I would lose every penny I ever made as a player. And only years later did I fully dig out of the hole.

Not often in life does someone see such a dramatic and almost instant change of fortune—going from having the world by the collar to flailing just to stay above water. That period was the most impactful of my life to date. A trial like that teaches you more about yourself and those around you than any other experience. And believe it or not, that failure became a success. In the end I learned more about my God, my faith, my family, and my true friends than I had in all my other life experiences combined.

It's easy to talk about your faith when everything seems to be going well. And a family feels tight and happy when you seem to have everything you need and want. When you're constantly in the limelight, it seems you have limitless true friends.

It shouldn't come as a surprise, but when you're staring failure in the face, you learn the truth—about yourself, your resolve, and who your real friends are. But the bigger win is a strengthened personal faith, a rock-solid marriage, and a real-life lesson to our kids about financial responsibility and the meaninglessness of mere "stuff."

Best of all, I now cherish a group of friends I would gladly follow into any foxhole.

I certainly wouldn't want to go through any of that again, but I thought you might want a glimpse behind the curtain that might have otherwise looked like a fairy-tale ride.

Has the same proven true for you—that as painful as the lows can be, in the end you became wiser in the process, even to where you can say, "I'm actually glad that happened to me"?

That being the case, why are we as adults afraid to let our own kids—and their teammates—face a little adversity? Maybe we need to resist our natural impulse to rescue everyone. Within reason, let them fail. After they have invested sweat and tears and the discipline of hard work to achieve something, and then failed in spite of it all, the lessons they learn can make them better people—and the odds are that they will eventually succeed. Imagine how much more it will mean to them then!

The life lessons they learn will be hard-won and result in skills that make them not only better teammates now but will also stick with them the rest of their lives. Win, lose, or draw, let them know you're proud of them. The wins or losses are secondary to all they've learned, so buy them some ice cream and help them grow, especially from their failures.

How to Best Relate to Your Players

I feel deeply fortunate to have a group of friends committed to helping me improve as a leader. The wisdom they've shared with me has helped me relate to players better and gain true balance in my life. One friend, former big-league outfielder and manager Clint Hurdle, sent me a blog post (https://churchleaders.com/author/ron-edmondson) by Ron Edmondson (a pastor). I found it packed with great concepts that can apply to any team, whether on a baseball field or in a boardroom. Take the time to check it out and share with your team Ron's twelve ways to become a valuable team member.

I try to teach my players a lot of other qualities that go into becoming a great teammate. Things like:

Humility
Hard work
Accountability

Reliability
Dependability
Promptness
Forthrightness (vocal when necessary)
Honesty
Trustworthiness
Empathy
Care
Competitiveness
Insight as opposed to cynicism
Optimism
Passion
Discipline

As you might imagine, the challenge for us coaches was to both live out the principles we were trying to teach and to also apply them in the heat of practices and games. I deeply sympathize with fathers whose prodigal children go their own ways, at least for a while. But many such parents admit that there was a disconnect between what they preached or tried to teach their kids and their own actions. It's one thing to harp on the need to prefer others over yourself but quite another to live that out in the privacy of your own home.

Too many prodigals point to the hypocrisy of their parents as one of the motivators for their straying from what they were taught. Admittedly, that's not always the case. Sometimes kids simply fall victim to peer pressure or succumb to their own selfishness. But most don't criticize their training; they just wish their parents had lived it out.

So my fellow coaches and I felt the weight of modeling what we were teaching, eager to train the boys in the game on the field and life off the field. We couldn't justify teaching servant leadership and then act like tyrants. We couldn't emphasize fun and learning over winning and then explode over losses.

The Best Time for Instruction

Let me reiterate that the ideal time for coaching is during practice and the repetitions kids are getting in at home. Coaching mechanical adjustments while they are in the batter's box is too little, too late. You might remind them of one cue before they go to the on-deck circle, but that's all. Better to let them take their at bat while you carefully observe and jot notes, then instruct them when they're back in the dugout. You can also give the boy and his parents homework between games.

Character Studies

How did all this play out from a practical standpoint? Every practice, we dedicated at least a half hour to character studies. We developed a template of detailed studies, which you can find here, covering such subjects as:

Character Studies

- Gratitude
- Self-discipline
- Courage
- Goals
- Community service
- Excellence
- Leadership
- Responsibility
- Teamwork
- Sportsmanship

Nonfaith
Character Studies

We discussed these concepts with even the youngest players. You should feel free to use these verbatim, if they seem to apply to your team—or adapt them as you feel it appropriate. If you're not comfortable coming at this from as faith-based an angle as we did, I have also linked to a supply of more generic topics. Feel free to use these as you please.

What Stuck with Players

"The routine ingrained in us from a young age helped us get the most out of what we were doing. Practices were intended to be fun too. I like that there was a hugely important theme to every practice. I was able to be with my friends and have fun while playing a sport I loved. As we grew up, we realized we loved each other and shared a deep desire to get better, to win, and grow deeper in character."

I used a little time at the end of each practice to conduct these. You don't have to do this on the field—you can do this anywhere. Be careful to keep these brief, because as important as they are, the kids should be pretty well spent and their attention spans may be short. Don't underestimate what these studies could mean to your team, especially if you're on the same page with me regarding what we're really trying to accomplish as coaches.

I was pleased to discover how well these studies stuck with our boys and how they still talk about them to this day. There are valuable life skills to be gleaned from these. Ten years will come and go quickly, and you'll find that you've made lifelong friends of young men you can be proud of—likely more because of the character studies than anything you taught them on the field.

I asked some of my former youth-league players to contribute how they felt about this at the time and how they feel about it now that they are adults.

Input from Former Youth-League Team Members

While the team members from more than a decade ago have asked to remain anonymous, what they share about all they learned warms me and my fellow coaches. They have permitted me to quote them here. One former player says, "The character studies helped me reflect and become mentally tough. Without them, it would have been hard to see why we are expected to act certain ways on the field and in life in general. I truly believe that learning those lessons at a young age helped prepare me to become a hard-working person with a positive attitude as a man. We were taught that the mind is one of the most important elements that contributes to being a good ballplayer and teammate, and the character studies helped reinforce that."

Another says, "Even as kids, our conversations became more serious and brought us together on a deeper level than just sports and baseball. We talked about important personal things like our faith, our family, our friends, and how important were the decisions we were making.

"I learned about loyalty, becoming mentally tough, the value of teamwork, and how crucial it is to become a person of integrity. It was a great way to get us all on the same page before we went out to practice. As I grew up I realized how this off-the-field training differentiated us from other teams. The coaches never apologized for trying to make us better men, even over making us better baseball players. That isn't saying they didn't care about the physical side of things. Just that if they could choose what to emphasize, ten times out of ten they would want to help make us better, well-rounded men."

Another says, "It's funny that after all the time we spent on character studies, I specifically remember one session the most—the one on setting goals. I still have somewhere my notes on that and the goals I set for myself as a youngster. And while all the rest of the character training seems to run together in my mind, somehow it worked. I learned to be a better person and more faith-filled through sports. I was surprised to learn that we could use sports to carry out God's will in our lives, but strange as that seemed, it reached me. I have been able to relate to and apply those character studies to life beyond baseball. The coaches made clear that life is bigger than baseball, and those character studies taught me how to treat others—a truth that still serves me well today."

Another says, "I learned things way bigger than baseball. While we eventually became competitive, we received so much more than skill development. We matured as human beings. We learned about how to conduct ourselves the right way, on and off the field, how to treat people, how to glorify God if that's what you wanted to do."

"Character studies were something I looked forward to the most," one says. "I had kind of a dicey home life, so it was a confusing time for me when I was really impressionable. The character studies proved incredibly beneficial because they were lessons taught outside of school and home. I was able to learn and understand who I wanted to be and to become. The lessons were broken down and explained in ways that made sense, to where I could clearly understand them and evaluate them for myself. To this day I still apply all the important lessons I learned."

I actually ran through a version of character studies every morning of spring training with our big leaguers. The first benefit is obvious: you invest in your players' values that will carry far beyond their days in a baseball uniform. Meanwhile, you're building a team culture around things that are important to you: what it looks like to be a young baseball player—and more importantly, a young man—with high character.

Lastly, these sessions have a way of keeping you and your coaching assistants accountable for how you handle yourselves on and off the field.

What Stuck with Players

"During our character studies we talked about what we learned, our attitudes, work ethics, lives, and even faith. We heard real-life life examples or read verses from the Bible and thought about situations that would be similar to playing a baseball game. That really helped us become mentally tough. Doing those at a young age helped form us into the hardworking, positive men we are today."

Ready for Some Baseball?

If you're like me, there comes a time near the end of winter when you start getting itchy to get back to baseball. Maybe your team is set, you've ordered uniforms to fit everyone, and you're getting to know the individual players. You may start to get panicky about what you're going to do with these kids, once it's time to put on the gloves and pick up the bats and really get started.

I want to walk you through what is expected of you, what you should expect of your assistant coaches, what you should expect of parents, and primarily what you should try to teach the kids in the way of specific baseball skills. That has consumed much of my adult life, so let me cover it with the help of a lot of trusted expert friends.

3

Keeping Parents Up to Speed

You've done your homework, thought through—at least somewhat—how you want to run your team, and perhaps you've even determined the kinds of character qualities you'd like to develop and instill in your players.

But for any of this to truly work, you need to build a strong relationship with your players' parents. That doesn't mean that you would, or should, always give in to them or even entertain all their input. But it does mean you need their buy-in to make your coaching effective and your lessons stick. That's my aim in this chapter—to help you accomplish that from day one, even when the going gets tough.

You're likely to run into lots of questions from your kids' parents, so it's best to be prepared and even head those off—answering them before they're asked, if possible. There are a few areas you'll want to be conversant about:

Things Parents Should Do and Not Do

As a Dad Coach, you can help other parents know what they should and should not do when practicing with their child at home. Without counsel, they'll likely fall into the trap of over-teaching. Rather than harping on "get your elbow up" or "keep your eye on the ball," the best input a parent can give is "Almost. Keep trying," and "Great try—you almost got that one."

I'm amazed at how the human body and mind figures out on its own what needs to be done, provided there is appropriate effort on the part of the player. That's why it can be counterproductive for parents to constantly try to instruct a kid in every aspect of his play. Better to let them figure things out on their own and not feel badgered about positioning their hands, telling them how to lean or jump or react to various types of throws or hits. Urge parents to keep encouraging while minimizing the instructing. Give them confidence that they can leave the coaching to you, and assure them that if there's something specific you need them to reinforce, you'll let them know.

The overcoached kid is easy to recognize. When he steps into the batter's box, he'll look into the stands to see if he's positioned correctly, if his elbow is at the right angle, and even if his jersey is tucked in and his pants are worn properly. You'll help this player by persuading his well-intentioned parents how hard the game is, even without worrying about five different mechanical cues before he tries to hit a thrown sphere with a round bat.

A question I frequently hear from parents is, "What's the most important thing I can do to help my child improve at baseball?" Many have told me they expected me to suggest they invest in private coaching or even fly their child to one of the great baseball camps in the country. But my answer? "Just play catch with them whenever you can." Repetitions are king for the young ballplayer. In the beginning stages, even a barehand underhand toss back and forth is important. Once the catches are made consistently with two hands, then challenge them to catch using only their glove hand without the glove. A glove can be added later, but barehand is a great start.

If you really make the effort to listen, you'll find that what our kids really want, more than anything, is the opportunity to spend time with us. A poignant story I heard recently went like this: A young boy asked his highly successful father how much he made per hour at work. The father proudly answered that he was paid about one hundred an hour. The boy asked if he could borrow fifty dollars. The father scolded him for asking and lectured him on how hard he works for that money.

The boy went to his room in tears, so his dad followed him to apologize and try to explain further. He found the boy on his bed counting a stack of singles and change. "What are you wanting to do with all that money?"

His son said, "I have saved up almost fifty dollars and wanted to borrow fifty more so I could pay for an hour to play catch with you."

If that doesn't make you want to grab a glove and head outside with your son, I don't know what will.

Go Outside and Play!

This is good counsel for parents, so never be afraid to advise it. But notice I did not say, "Send them outside to play."

For too many parents, it's been a long time since they went outside to play a game *with* their kids. I know everybody gets so busy that going outside to play with our kids doesn't seem feasible. Let me challenge you and urge you to challenge the other parents to make some changes. Kids today stay inside way too much.

I'm guessing that some of your greatest childhood memories

are similar to mine. My dad and I used to go outside and . . . You fill in the rest. My favorite memories involve my family outdoors, either making up games in the backyard or going hunting and fishing. I believe all that time outside helped me develop the physical skills that allowed me to play at higher levels. But even more importantly, it was just plain fun. Our biggest concern was how much longer we could play before dark.

So, what's changed? The kids or us parents?

It's easy to let kids drift into a video-game coma so we can get all our "important things" done. But ask kids if they would like to go outside and play a game of one-on-one hoops or throw the ball around. I think we all know how most would respond.

You may say your kids are too old now and you missed your chance. Well, if it's true that the best time to plant a tree is twenty years ago, the second-best time is right now. Start a new tradition. Whether your kids are teenagers or toddlers, go outside and play!

How Many Lessons Are Enough?

In my early teens it became obvious that I was a good baseball player. Looking back on it, I can see that one of the greatest gifts my parents gave me was never forcing me to take lessons. Even more surprising, my father never jammed his baseball knowledge down my throat. He has always been an avid baseball fan. In fact, as a kid himself he left the family farm in Mason County, West Virginia, to chase his dream of playing professional baseball. He had a couple of tryouts with big-league clubs, but nothing ever came of it.

Still, his passion for the game was obvious, and he passed that on to my brothers and me. He was an ideal youth-league coach because he was always positive, knowing when to instruct and when to let us figure it out on our own. When he pitched batting practice, he would study my swing, but he rarely offered anything but compliments. He just kept pitching, brilliantly advising me to learn what a good swing felt like and to not think too much. "Just see it and hit it."

I somehow forgot that counsel as the years passed and I played under more and more coaches. By the time I reached professional baseball, I had lost what a good swing felt like. I became so accustomed to hitting coaches telling me how to hold my hands and what my stride should look like that I had turned into a robot at the plate. I concentrated so much on mechanics that I forgot my father's advice. I still made it to the major leagues, mostly because I could catch and throw, but hitting became misery for me.

I'm not saying I didn't have some great hitting coaches. All of them just wanted to see me succeed, and I was nothing if not coachable. The problem was that I couldn't separate all the mechanics from what I was trying to do in the game—just put the ball in play. I see the same thing with many young players today. They go through ten different routines in the batter's box before they even look up at the pitcher.

You'll want to try to help parents avoid this trap, especially those who don't have much baseball experience. I'm not saying to avoid hitting lessons, as most kids could use help with their swings. Just don't let your players be force-fed mechanics. They should walk to the plate excited about trying to do the hardest thing in sports. The bottom line is, hitting is hard. You and your coaches and their parents can help your kids the most by throwing them lots of pitches, with little to no instruction. You'll be amazed at how they figure it out on their own, and the game will become more enjoyable for both of you.

Communicating with Parents

You might find the coach-parent relationship delicate, so let me clarify that there will be things I advise you to do with them and things I would urge you to not do. I'm already clearly on record how important it is to establish from the get-go that youth-league baseball must be all about the kids, not the parents. I even let parents know that I'm not available for conversations right after a game. Frankly, that's a train wreck waiting to happen. Even if they just want to compliment you, you're best off to just thank them and be on your way. If you don't, you'll soon face a crowd of parents—and they won't all be complimenting you. Some may pretend to do that while actually angling for you to favor their kid.

Obviously you want parents to trust you and be on your side, but you'll be amazed how quickly things can spiral out of control. If you allow it, you'll find that most nightmare conversations with parents happen after a game when emotions are raw and feelings are hurt. Like never before, parents are incredibly sensitive if they believe their child has been treated unfairly in any way. And I'm not talking about something actually blatant, as in your having lost your temper, perhaps raised your voice, that kind of thing. In those cases, parents have a right to confront you, and you should be prepared to sincerely apologize.

But I've also seen cases where a parent gets upset about their kid's spot in the batting order, the position he was asked to play, even whether he was given a bunt sign when they believe he's a power hitter who should have been allowed to hit away. That's when you need to remind them that they agreed to not interfere with coaching decisions and that if they're truly unhappy about that, they might be better off having their child play for another team.

I know that can come off as harsh, but if you establish the ground rules from the beginning, you've laid the foundation for procedures that must be followed.

There are all kinds of ways to communicate with parents these days, including apps that announce practice and games schedules, allow for online electronic fee collection, and can even be programmed to inform the kids whether they're to wear their home or away jersey for a particular game. Here's a QR code linking to that app, which you might find useful. It's not mandatory that you use it, but at least check it out. Even if you don't consider yourself app-savvy, it's fairly self-explanatory. One of the kids or one of your assistant coaches might be assigned to access it and use it.

Scheduling App

I recommend limiting the number of times you'll meet with all the parents after a game. You might restrict it to when you're planning a road trip to a tournament or something like that, where it's important everyone is on the same page. Because it's after a game, you'll want to keep any comments about that game strictly positive and leave individual player names out of your comments—even the ones you praise. Otherwise, someone is sure to feel jealous or left out. Rather, that would be the ideal time to praise the team as a whole—whether you've won or lost. In those instances I would say something like, "I'm really proud of how hard the boys played today. They're putting in a high level of effort in practices and in games, and I see us improving every day."

Then, to both compliment the diligent parents and motivate the others, I might say, "It's obvious that many of you are playing catch with your kids at home, as they're getting better at catching the ball in the air and catching grounders. Have them keep working on their accuracy by throwing to a spot on the wall or giving them a target when you're playing catch with them. Once again, you want to balance challenge with success."

Tell parents of the youngest-age players to encourage their sons to throw a big ball off the wall and see how many times they can catch it with two hands. Quickly, hand-eye coordination will turn into the desire for more challenge. Playing Wiffle ball or a softball-sized plastic or foam ball is a good next step, and start with a big plastic bat.

Parents should be advised to avoid jumping right into playing catch with their kids with real baseballs. Two things can happen before the player is prepared for the hard ball: they may get hit and begin to fear the ball, or they become bored trying to hit inaccurate pitches (no offense to parents, but it is sometimes hard to hit a young player's bat with your pitches).

You can also tell parents that hitting practice at home is good for everybody. They can have their sons hit off a tee or make a soft-toss blanket they can hit into. This can be done inside with a Wiffle ball, even golf-ball-sized Wiffle balls, anything that will help with eye-hand coordination and bat-to-ball skills. Be sure to thank them for supporting the kids and helping them grow in their passion for the game.

You might find it strange that a former big-league catcher and manager is a huge proponent of what many consider just a fun, silly diversion like this. But I am. In fact, I've actually had Wiffle ball fields constructed on my property. It became a great family game, and believe it or not, many big leaguers have played Wiffle at our place. It's a fun and effective way for parents to get their kids a lot of hitting repetitions.

I also encourage parents to watch big-league games on TV with their kids and talk about what happens, what should have happened, what mistakes were made. Get them critically thinking about baseball.

One thing I would encourage you *not* to do is allow too much email between you and the parents. They should be able to get all the information they need from the app. If you're uncomfortable managing the app and can't find an assistant or even a player who can handle that for you, at least find someone who can get your schedule and frequently asked questions posted somewhere online so parents can easily access it. Believe me, you might otherwise spend half your coaching time answering myriad questions from parents.

In those rare cases when parents overstep and complain, griping about their kid's playing time or positioning, you may have to cut ties with the family. I hate that a kid suffers because his parents can't control themselves, and I try to avoid that at all costs. But making such a hard decision can also save you some heartache down the road. Other families will catch on that you mean what you say.

If you're willing and have the time, you might establish a certain time every few weeks where you announce that you'll be available online for parents to contact you. But it's crucial you set boundaries so they're asking generally about traveling or game logistics and don't resort to lobbying for their player's individual wishes.

Now, if several families start removing their kids from your team, obviously it's time for you to conduct a little introspection. No one wants a reputation for being an Eeyore as a coach. Remind yourself of the Competitive EDGES from chapter 1, especially the E-Flywheel (Enthusiasm, Energy, and Encouragement), and your players will want to be around you.

The Miserable Car Ride Home

The results of a thirty-year survey of collegians may surprise you. Asked, "What was the worst thing about playing sports as a kid?" the overwhelming answer was, "The car ride home with my parents."

Ouch!

The study also showed that the major offenders were not the whacked-out, over-the-top screamers, but parents who typically kept quiet during the game. Once in the car, they could no longer control their frustration.

The study also noted that nearly 70 percent of the kids quit their sport by the time they were thirteen, due to a fractured relationship with their parents. Some even stated that they believed they could get their parents back to normal by quitting the sport altogether. How sad—parents risking their relationship with their kids, just to give them advice before they even take off their jersey.

The solution? The kids in the survey said the greatest thing their parents could tell them after a game was, "I loved watching you play."

Kids do not want to hear that their coach was wrong, or the ump was blind, or that they should not have thrown a 3-2 change-up. They just want to know we enjoy watching them.

So, you are likely to run into the occasional parent who thinks their kid is better than he actually is. I get that. We can all tend to see our kids through rose-colored glasses. But the parents you want to beware of are those prone to challenge your decisions—or worse, your whole new coaching philosophy—whenever they get the chance.

If they're not taking into consideration the overall team strategy for both learning and fun, their going to bat for their kid is almost always parent-initiated rather than player-initiated. This seems to be more prevalent in this era of entitlement. Yes, we parents are wired to believe our number one job is to protect and defend our kids. It's really healthier if they learn to let the youngsters start fending for themselves at the proper time.

That's why I emphasize clearly setting precedents and expectations from the very beginning. You're asking—actually insisting—that parents agree to entrust their child to your team and to you. Once they've agreed to that, they must follow the guidelines. Make crystal clear your motive: to help every player without favoritism.

List your nonnegotiables: equal distribution of playing time, positioning, and batting order. These issues will potentially bring you more parental grief than anything else. Especially for the earliest ages, I recommend what I call the "rubber band" theory. For your first game of the season, simply have the players hit in the order of their defensive positions (Pitcher 1, catcher 2, first base 3, second base 4, third base 5, shortstop 6, left field 7, center field 8, right field 9), and then your extra hitters (if your league allows or requires this) in jersey numerical order.

If, say, your left fielder (7) makes the final out of the game, the next hitter will bat first in the next game, and so on, through the remainder of the season—or at least as long as it takes for you to settle on the most competitive batting order—still allowing everyone the same amount of playing time.

I propose rotating the boys around the field, playing a new position at least every game but often within the same game. Some argue that they won't learn one position if they don't concentrate on it for several games, but I contend it's more important, especially for the 6–8 year-olds, to learn all the positions. The goal, again, is fun. It should also present them a little challenge. This should actually keep the parents happy, because the boys really don't care where they play or where they hit in the order until they hear their parents complaining.

What Stuck with Players

"At practice we were expected to get our work done and learn about the game while also having fun. Even when we didn't realize it, we were slowly getting better through repetition and little competitions."

Keep the rotation simple and predictable. A kid should move from pitcher to catcher to first, to second, to third, etc. If anyone has a true fear of catching, work around that by allowing the boys who are interested in it to give it a shot. By the time a kid has reached right field in his rotation, he should then take his turn on the bench. This is especially important during tee-ball or coaches-pitch seasons.

These are things parents should simply not contact you about, even as they progress to the age where you're using a more strategic approach to setting the batting order. If the player himself struggles with any of this, *he,* not mom or dad, should be the one to approach you and ask the questions. Maybe it's, "Coach, why am I always the last batter?" That becomes your opportunity to acknowledge how difficult that can be for a young player and explain as forthrightly as possible both the reason and, more importantly, what the player can do to change his circumstances. Sure, for the youngest players at the earliest stages, you have a simple explanation of how the batting order is established—mostly random, sometimes alphabetically, sometimes by position, etc. But as the kids mature and the season progresses and you begin arranging the batting order strategically, your answer can change.

Feel free to be forthright. You can tell a kid, "For you to rise in the batting order, I need to see you improve on your bunting . . ." or "I'd like to see you making more contact . . ." Suggest drills he can do at home to improve. Most kids rise to the challenge and feel valued by such honest input.

This may sound a little idealistic, but incredible things can happen in a kid's development if they learn to take this mature approach. They're showing a willingness to learn and grow, not just to gripe or beg. If parents insist on taking matters into their own hands, they're depriving their child of a great learning opportunity. Just remember, coach, that much of this is your responsibility. It is about the kids and their development as people, not about winning trophies.

> "The expectations of us during games was pretty clear and simple. You were going to give one hundred percent whether you were playing shortstop or left bench. We were taught that there were four things we could control—Attitude, Concentration, Effort, and Selflessness (ACES)."

Club Teams

More and more parents seem to ask me—and you'll get these questions too—about the value and importance of their child playing on a club team. Everybody seems aware of the potential upside: playing with the best players in town, traveling, getting noticed in tournaments, and all the rest. The concept is not bad in general, but be prepared to tell parents of the downside too. The fact is that a club team can be a terrible fit for some kids and their families.

Regular youth leagues are expensive enough. But a club team? The cost per player can be astronomical. There are travel and lodging costs, equipment costs, tournament fees, you name it. But some hear stories of some one-in-a-million kid whose parents remortgaged their house or took on a side hustle so they could afford this, and their son wound up getting a scholarship or even drafted into the pros.

So, yes, for some minuscule fraction of all the club team players, their kid makes it all worth it in the end. But the fact is that the odds are about the same as winning the lottery. Some of the best natural athletes ever—whose horizons appeared limitless—blew out a knee or an arm and were never heard from again.

The problem is that many adults fear they're not being the best parents they can be if they're not getting their child to the most sought-after team in town. But when they stretch beyond their means to accomplish this, the pressure to see a return on that investment eventually rolls down to the player. That's an awful lot of tension to put on a kid.

You can also remind parents that pushing their child beyond his ability level can result in him spending most of his time on the bench. Better to find an appropriate level of competition where he sees a lot of playing time and progresses rather than regresses in his development.

Some club team coaches will warn parents that the only way their son will make it to the next level is "if he plays on this team." The fact is that if their son can play, they'll be discovered. As they get older, do they sometimes need help getting exposed? Yes, and there are ways that you can do that within a budget.

Where this gets ridiculous is when clubs start making their way down to the parents of kids at the youngest ages and assuring them that their particular club sees 80 percent of their kids make it into Division 1 schools. The implication, of course, is that the only way for your child to be seen by college recruiters is to start them at the lowest level in their club system.

Frankly, that's just garbage. So many guys on my big-league teams, and in the minor-league system, played only recreationally until they got into high school. Then they had plenty of teams to choose from that would get them exposed.

Let me be clear: The idea of a club team works for some, and there are some great clubs doing it right—making strong efforts to get the kids the best instruction that they can and allowing them to play against the best competition in the area, while not trying to fleece every penny from the parents. It might not be easy to determine up front, but urge parents to be on the lookout for teams that seem to emphasize expensive uniforms and equipment over what the kids are really learning. If a family can afford it, the child is begging for more baseball, and he's talented enough to get playing time on a club team, I'm not against it. But if any of those conditions don't describe a kid or his family, assure them they should keep looking and not settle for a team just because it looks cool or is popular.

4

Earning the Right to Be Heard

While it's true that most players on a new team want to put their best foot forward and impress the coach—hoping, of course, to get a lot of playing time—it's not uncommon for some to withhold their enthusiasm for their coaches until they see what they have to offer. This may be subtle to detect, but they're basically silently challenging you to prove yourself. So one of the upsides of being prepared—with all the training videos and the tightly packed practice schedule—is that it quickly earns you the right to be heard.

That's no small gift from players. Maybe we'd love it if they simply showed respect for their elders, the way we were expected to when we were kids. And some will. But today you need to build trust with your players and their parents—and that's not a bad thing. As soon as you have won over the born skeptics and outliers, use that rapport in the best way possible. Disabuse them of some popular but mythical so-called truths permeating youth sports today.

One of the first is that there is some merit in quickly becoming a one-sport specialist and often even a one-position baseball player. The thinking goes that this is the quickest way to stand

What Stuck with Players

"We were expected to respond to our elders with respect. Everything was, 'Yes, sir,' and 'No, sir,' as we learned to be coachable."

out, get noticed, and get oneself in line for elite traveling teams, scholarships, even professional ball. Besides the fact that we've already established that such success is limited to an extremely minuscule minority anyway, the thinking itself is flawed.

I've actually run into parents who insist that their kid be labeled as a PO (Pitcher Only). One sport. One position. And don't get in the way of his development.

After years in the big leagues as a player, a talent evaluator, and a manager, I know the folly of this thinking. Almost every Major League Baseball player was a multisport participant and even credits that variety for much of his success. Players who limit themselves, or allow themselves to be limited, to a single sport often eventually hit a wall. The game becomes a grind, no longer fun. They burn out on it and sometimes turn their back on it forever. That's a tragedy.

Sports are supposed to be fun and challenging, something you enjoy even during the tough times. The way to ensure that is to broaden your horizons, not narrow them. When baseball season is over, kids should pick another sport they like. Learn teamwork, discipline, consistency, and have fun. If eventually baseball becomes a singular pursuit, it should be *because,* not *in spite of,* what they learned from other sports.

> **What Stuck with Players**
>
> "The expectation was that we would show up to practice on time and be ready to go. Once we were done with the character studies, we were to be dialed in and focused on practicing for the next hour or ninety minutes. I admit it was an adjustment at first, because we were expected to listen and be ready at whatever station we were assigned and not be goofing off. That kind of discipline, along with the character studies, was different from the way we'd been coached before. We had to focus, and there was no standing around."

For one thing, kids will develop faster athletically. And who knows? They might discover a sport they love even more and want to concentrate on that.

There is no question that I would have burnt out at an early age, and probably peaked too soon, if I had played only baseball. I love the change of seasons the same way I loved the change from football in the fall to basketball in the winter to baseball in the spring and summer. The variety kept me passionate about all three sports. In the fall, I wanted to be Roger Staubach more than anything in the world. Even while shoveling snow off the basketball courts in the winter, I dreamt of playing like Larry Bird in college. As soon as spring rolled around, I wanted to be Johnny Bench.

It hurts me today to see kids go from spring baseball to summer baseball travel season to a fall baseball league, and then spend their entire winter in a rigorous baseball training program—all at a young age. Aside from the mental exhaustion that often results, there can also be physical repercussions from the repetitions and workload. Leading orthopedic surgeons agree that extensive repetitive movements increase the likelihood of injuries requiring surgical repair. Why subject kids to such a prospect?

I've come to believe it's much more important to develop young athletes holistically. Legendary college basketball coach Bobby Knight once told me that he made a point to watch his potential recruits play a sport other than basketball, because he was looking for certain traits. First, he wanted to see how they moved in another sport. The question was whether they were just as athletic on a field of play other than the basketball court. He already knew the recruit would stand out on the hardwood, or he wouldn't have been pursuing him in the first place. But how did a 6'6" power forward perform on the baseball field? Would this player fight and compete as much to stand out in a secondary sport as he did in basketball?

Secondly, Coach Knight told me he feared the "basketball-only" athlete was at a higher risk of max-out or burnout. We know what burnout is, but what is max-out? It's simply when a young player may have had so much instruction and repetition that he might not be able to improve enough to compete at the next level.

So players can max out *or* burn out, due to specialization and overexposure. The question is, who is at fault? Is the engine pushing this train the athlete himself, or is it an overconscientious parent or coach trying to force onto a kid an adult mentality of discipline and commitment? I say let the kids chase fun for now and the rest will sort itself out in due time.

What did I learn from the other sports I played? Basketball taught me a different type of eye-hand coordination than baseball did. Plus I learned endurance from running up and down the court. Then there was first-step quickness. I was forced to train my nondominant hand. I may have been tall enough and just about right for baseball, but not for basketball. I had to counter my height disadvantage by playing pickup games with kids much older than me. Learning to compete with them taught me toughness, and also often how to lose with grace and class. Playground basketball courts can be rough places, so I had to learn that the hard way. My first fistfight was on a basketball court with a kid two years older than me.

One advantage with basketball is that we could play one-on-one if we had to. With baseball you really need at least four people to have a game. I learned to handle the pressure on the free-throw line with all eyes on you. Basketball also taught me teamwork and the value of passing and assists.

Football taught me toughness and resilience. I learned to physically push myself beyond what I thought were my limits. I learned how to deal with angry coaches. I learned the importance of strength training. I learned leadership as a quarterback. I actually developed a pass-release slot that worked with how I needed to throw as a catcher. I learned to take a hit, which was also an important part of the catching game at the time. I learned how to put a hit on someone else, which was also part of baseball back then. I benefited from specific coaching on speed and agility. I learned teamwork at an even deeper level than the other sports, as there were more players, a more diversified group from all socioeconomic backgrounds, all working together as one.

Your team is listening to you, so advise them to play as many sports as they want to. They'll be glad they did.

Another way to earn the right to be heard comes in the form of a gift you can offer the kids and their parents, and that is to keep your word and start and end practice on time. The more you do this and the more you stay vigilant about maximizing every minute, the better your team will become.

Hustle is a nonnegotiable, and hard work should be praised. In the business world you often hear that "employees will respect what you inspect." In other words, if they know you're watching and noticing results, they'll strive even more to perform and deliver. In baseball, it's even simpler. I find that players of any age will repeat what you praise. That's why it's also important to have a specific *Why* for each drill, and make it plain. "This is important because . . ."

One thing to watch for, once you've earned your team's attention, is developing cliques. Sure, you want kids to become friends, and some will be drawn to certain teammates and not so much to others. But cliques in practice and on the field should be broken up. Rearrange the groups at the next practice; get the more advanced players to help the less advanced. Be intentional about who goes into each group and watch them gel.

A perfect example of this is Adam Wainwright. The 6'7", 230-pound veteran ace of the St. Louis Cardinals was a joy to manage because he was a warrior on the mound. He was a Cy Young–caliber starter and battled back from Tommy John ligament replacement surgery. But the value of a player like Waino goes way beyond the wins and losses. He could have become aloof, played the big shot, knowing he was our ace for many years. But he didn't. That was not who Waino was.

I found in him more than just a great pitcher, but also a man with the ability and the willingness to speak to many players and to help bring them along, due to his experience and his incomparable work ethic. I didn't need to badger the team to listen to Adam. His leadership was unmistakable. He was a stand-up guy in our clubhouse and out in the community. He kept guys loose even when it was not his day to pitch, and when it was his day, he proved fiercely competitive and focused. The guys admired and respected the pitcher and the person.

All that is to say, I carefully selected who would be in Wainwright's group for spring training drills. Just being around him made them more conscientious. Nobody stood around with him. The contrast would have been glaring. Even after I moved on from the Cardinals, I was thrilled to see Waino prove all the naysayers wrong when it appeared his career was over. He suffered the usual aches and pains and injuries that veterans do, and it seemed every week one so-called expert or another was predicting the end for him. And that was years ago, even before he turned forty. At forty-one, he was chosen to start the USA's opening game in the World Baseball Classic. Amazing.

Pitcher Chris Carpenter was another respected competitor and beloved Cardinal who went out of his way to make people around him better. He came to St. Louis after six seasons with Toronto and became our ace. But his legacy goes beyond his three All-Star Game appearances, one Cy Young Award, and two World Series championships. Like Adam Wainwright who followed him, Carp modeled a unique work ethic and a fiery competitiveness. The many pitchers in St. Louis fortunate enough to spend time with him were learning from one of the best.

He had a hard time with the news that his shoulder rehab had not progressed the way he had hoped and that he would have to leave the game. I asked him if there was anything he wanted me to say to the fans during the press conference announcing his retirement, and he took a long pause. Finally he said, "Just that I'm sorry I let you all down."

All I could think of was, *Are you kidding me?* But that was vintage Carp. This guy once had a rib removed and pitched a couple of months later just because he knew we needed him. He fought through countless other surgeries, always focusing on getting back to the team. He's the epitome of a model teammate.

Carp was a quiet leader, one of the best. His dedicated work ethic clearly made everyone else better. Watch for those quiet leaders on your team and be sure to put the younger or more impressionable guys with them.

Section Two

Making Practice Perfect (or Close to It)

5

Logistics

What You Need Before You Step on the Field

When I take on a project, any kind of a challenge really, I want to be ready. Don't you? The job you've accepted is huge. You want to successfully lead the kids under your charge to succeed on and off the baseball field. That takes preparation, planning, and serious thought.

Choosing Your Coaches

So where do you start? By getting help. You can't do this alone.

You're looking for certain qualities, of course, but primarily, you want assistant coaches who share your philosophy. You need to be able to talk frankly with them about the character you're looking for. Don't confuse the kids by modeling your best self while allowing assistant coaches to model something else entirely.

Admittedly, one of the trickiest parts of assembling a coaching squad is that usually each of you will have at least one son on the team. It's vital from the beginning to establish that coaches must not favor—or perhaps worse—pick on their own kids. I've seen it happen both ways. Either way, when a father's love for his son, and desire for him to succeed, prevent him from focusing on the rest of the players' needs, the whole team suffers.

A goal of youth-league coaches should be to make it impossible for outsiders to know which kid is theirs. Everyone should be treated equally. That doesn't mean they'll all be treated the same, because you'll eventually learn who responds best to what kind of an approach. Just be sure you're basing your coaching on their makeup and sensibilities.

So where do you find like-minded coaches? You might not, in which case you'll have to educate them. But it's likely they'll agree with the approach I recommend. That was one of the upsides of *The Matheny Manifesto*. It resonated with so many parents and coaches that it gave me hope for the future of youth-league coaching. Even people who had gotten caught up in the winning-at-all-cost mentality seemed to quickly catch on to the idea of a commitment to character-molding.

Ideally, you'd want three assistant coaches—a bench coach and two base coaches—but if three proves to be a luxury, you could also assume one of those roles yourself. And, of course, each coach would also have other responsibilities. You'd want someone to work with your pitchers and catchers, someone to take charge of infield drills and workouts, and someone else for the outfield. But still it's helpful to have a coach for various positions and hitting and baserunning.

I recognize that few youth-league teams have coaches who have played professional baseball, but I was determined to not let my experience lead to unrealistic expectations on the parts of parents and players. Yes, I was also fortunate enough to recruit former big leaguer John Mabry as one of my assistants, and he also happened to have a son on the team. But we quickly disabused other parents of the notion that we were going to field a team of superstars with all the equipment to make them look like miniature pros.

Oh, we faced teams that would show up with expensive bat bags, several home and road uniforms patterned after big-league teams, and all the rest. With our emphasis on learning, growing, and building character, we provided our team with one pullover shirt for home games and another for away games. I never saw a fancy uniform or expensive equipment win a ball game or build character.

Having the right assistants will make your job a lot easier, especially if you develop an atmosphere of in-game accountability. More on that later, but it's what keeps baseball from becoming boring, especially for kids temporarily on the bench.

So, while I recommend you have at least two assistants—and ideally three—I do not advise more than that. Kids learn things in steps, and if they're getting input from too many directions at once, overcoaching can prove counterproductive.

It's great if your assistants have some baseball experience, but any athletic experience or understanding of teamwork and coaching hierarchy (letting the head coach be the head coach) is valuable. Obviously, they must understand the commitment required to do this right. Most important, whether or not you find coaches with the right experience and knowledge, is that you're careful to sift out the hotheads. I wish I could think of a more delicate way to say that, but you simply must avoid bringing on assistants who don't understand what's become widely known as servant leadership.

Good coaches, like good CEOs in the business world, serve from the bottom up rather than the top down. They listen as much as they talk. They're in charge and accept the responsibility of making the tough decisions. But they base those decisions on input from the people on their teams.

Maybe the analogy weakens a bit when we're talking about input from kids ages six through twelve, but the principle remains sound. You don't just boss 'em around because you're in authority. You strive to nurture, to make them the best they can be—in baseball and in life.

When I was evaluating parents who might make good assistant coaches, I found myself wary of those who wanted to show off all their baseball knowledge every time I talked with them. But I appreciated the guys who lit up when we started talking about character development.

An obvious no-go as a potential assistant coach was the father of a first baseman who parked himself just outside the fence as close to his son as possible. This man was rightly proud to have an older son who was a Division 1 scholarship first baseman, and naturally he wanted the same for his younger son. So how did he go about encouraging him? He loudly coached his son from his folding chair, criticizing every catch, throw, or tag. He'd holler for his son to slap hard tags on baserunners diving back in, even calling out, "Rip his head off!"

Claiming to be a knowledgeable baseball man, he was always angling for a coaching job. The longer he was ignored, the angrier—and louder—he grew. Eventually his young son lost his heart for the game. It should be obvious that that's the kind of father to avoid. They take all the joy and fun out of the game for a kid desperate to please his dad and to the detriment of the team and his passion for the game.

All right, you have your job, know your role, have your priorities in order, and you've recruited some help. Be sure your assistant coaches are people committed to every practice and every game. There will obviously be occasional exceptions, but they need to know the expectations. Tell them you'll coordinate and organize and run the workouts, but that you need their help to make the practices and pregame drills work efficiently.

Getting the Right Equipment

You're likely going to recoil at the cost of equipment. It's gotten out of hand, and even worse than the price tags is that most of these young athletes will outgrow their gear within the next year. But stay with me for a few things you can do to keep some costs down.

Mitts

I'll never forget the drive to Roush Sporting Goods in Columbus, Ohio, for the first catcher's mitt my dad bought me. I was so excited that the drive seemed to take forever. I chose a Rawlings mitt with a removable pad in the pocket to lessen the sting of an imperfect catch. I fell more in love with the game the day I was given that unique-smelling work of leather artistry I knew my dad had to save up for. That just made it all the more special. I slept with that glove under my bed for an entire spring, because someone told me that was how you break them in. The glove eventually broke in, and I used it until it fell apart.

Purchasing a glove can be overwhelming, but these days there are handy online charts to help you and your players understand the sizes of gloves used by players at different positions. Scan the QR code at right for a comprehensive chart for gloves, bats, and other equipment with sizing suggestions from Worth/Rawlings.

Rawlings Website

The youngest kids will most likely use the same glove for all positions, even catcher, during tee ball or coach pitch. If you're coaching 10–12 year-olds, look into a first baseman's mitt and a catcher's mitt for the team if none of the boys have one. And of course, outfielders use bigger gloves than infielders so they can gather in the ball after a long run. Infielders need a glove small enough to allow them to quickly transfer the ball to their throwing hand. These don't have to be brand-new and probably shouldn't be, as a brand-new glove can be miserable to learn with. Secondhand sports stores should have plenty of affordable options. Big and floppy will catch more balls than stiff and shiny.

I recommend kids getting one big enough for a ball to stay in the pocket but not so big that the glove won't stay on their hand.

Breaking in a New Glove

If you go the new mitt route, the next step is breaking it in. Here's a short video with tips for doing that. (My "sleeping with it under your bed" method from my youth isn't recommended.) I have used these methods many times with both catcher's mitts and fielder's mitts, as I try to shape the leather into the mold I like.

Footwear

Cleats are nice but not a necessity, since they're so quickly grown out of. Take the pressure off your kids' parents by simply having everyone wear black shoes or cleats. They're easy to find and match, and they offer everyone an affordable option.

Uniforms

Our team could afford nice jerseys, but we didn't see the point. For our first season, the parents paid for each player to be issued one T-shirt silk-screened with our team logo and their last name and number on the back and one pair of white uniform pants with an elastic belt to match the shirt.

We had one adjustable hat per player, and I always had a couple extras for every game since someone always forgot theirs. They used a Magic Marker to write their number on the underside of the bill, just like major leaguers do.

As your team gets older you can upgrade to two T-shirt jerseys in case you play a doubleheader, and two pairs of pants in case you have multiple games in a weekend. Nobody wanted to be scrubbing pants.

I never gave the boys grief for wearing dirt- or grass-stained pants, because they're so hard to keep clean. One season, we actually taught the boys how to wash their own pants and told them it was their responsibility. That didn't prove to be a favorite bit of advice.

Here are tips from a friend who helps out in a major-league clubhouse. Believe it or not, the pants are all hand-scrubbed each night by guys relentlessly working for hours and who do an amazing job.

Cleaning Uniforms

Among my favorite memories is walking my little ballplayers into a game where the opponent had embroidered uniforms and hats with custom piping and everything matching, from bags to shoes. My guys in their ten-dollar T-shirts often put a royal whupping on them.

So, do yourself and your team and the parents a favor, and don't sweat the petty stuff. Save your money for experiences that draw you and your players closer to each other, like field trips, team picnics, community projects, and so forth. You'll be amazed at how such bonding experiences will make the kids fall in love with the game more than a fancy uniform ever could.

Equipment for You

You will find a simple, inexpensive magnetic whiteboard a valuable tool. You can find these at an office supply store or online. I have one with hooks already attached so I can hang it anywhere, and I use magnets to show the various positions on the baseball field. I also have a magnetic whiteboard with a sticker in the shape of a baseball diamond. Paper names slide into magnetic strips so I can display who's playing where, and I can also show the batting order. Of course you can also do all this with just a whiteboard and no magnets.

Magnetic Whiteboards

You'll want to put one of these boards in the dugout where everyone can see it, and one of your assistant coaches should be in charge of keeping the boys moving to their next position and also show who is up to bat next. This is especially handy for the younger ages when you're rotating everyone through all the positions.

What Stuck with Players

"At first I didn't like the idea of rotations through various positions. I wanted to specialize. But in the end I saw how important it was that we experience as many positions as we could in order to decide what we liked best. And learning to play multiple positions made each of us a better asset to the team, more of a team player."

Scheduling

As I mentioned earlier, the app world has made amazing advancements in the options for youth sports. (By the time this book is released, anything I suggest here could be already passé. So do an internet search for the latest and greatest.) GameChanger, an app that calls itself "the one app for every baseball team," can actually handle scorekeeping, live video streaming, and team management. It's been at the forefront of sharing live scores and video coverage for families and fans who want to tune in from afar. But even aside from that, the real benefit is team management.

LeagueApps and TeamSnap can consolidate practice and game schedules and team communications. They even have options that accept payments, uniform selections, and a variety of other features to help take some of the load off you as the Dad Coach.

Where It Starts to Get Fun

Your adrenaline should start pumping when you announce your first practice, because this is where the rubber meets the road. You'll want to see your whole team, evaluate what and whom you have to work with, and really start getting to know the individual personalities.

That can all start with your first practice, where you must set the tone.

6

Before the Games Begin

Don't feel lonely if you're starting to get my drift that coaching, even at the youth-league level, is way more involved than just babysitting kids and playing a little baseball. I assume you're reading this because you want to do it right—or because a loved one knew you got roped into this job and hopes *The Dad Coach* can help.

You're not alone. In fact that same overwhelm you're feeling before your first actual practice is shared by even the most veteran of big-league managers every year. There's simply so much to be done, so much to remember, so many people to take care of.

Now is when you and your assistant coaches will want to access the links in this book that will take you to all the training videos you could ask for. Immerse yourselves in these and your kids will be impressed that you know what you're talking about and what you expect of them.

So what follows is what you need to prepare for during the season and after.

You've scheduled that first practice. You and your assistants and the kids will be there. You'll have your equipment. You'll give your foundational speech. Then what?

Well, while this is not complicated, it does have lots of moving parts, and it's crucial you plan to redeem the time. And I mean every minute of the time. You've clarified with the parents and guardians how long you'll have their kids for practice, and believe me, the time will fly. I urge you to start on time, end on time, and make sure *everyone* knows what they're to do all the time.

Positioning and Backup Responsibilities

Every player wants to be involved in every play, and it's our job as Dad Coaches to teach them that they do have a responsibility, whether they're directly involved or not. The video linked here will show you and your assistant coaches how to keep every kid on the field engaged. As you will see, I show many possible scenarios that may occur during a game. This is where your assistant coaches come into play. It's impossible to watch all nine players and hold them accountable for where they should be. One coach should supervise the pitcher and catcher while another coach is helping the infielders and another the outfielders.

Fielder Responsibilities

"It was mental mistakes or lack of effort we were to avoid at all cost. That's why we had to concentrate so hard on the game even when we were riding the bench. We were to be as involved in the game from the dugout as we were on the field and always ready to go when needed."

Tryouts

If you coach a team for a few years, you will inevitably have some churn in your roster. When you're looking for new players—assuming your league allows you to build your own team—I suggest reframing your tryouts by viewing them as not just talent scouting but also interviewing parents. Spend as much time as you can with the parents of a prospective player to see if they align with your expectations and priorities.

Also, look to shore up any deficiencies your team has. You need a good catcher, and you can never have too much pitching. If you just need bodies, start the interview process and do a little research. A typical practice session should give you a good idea how attentive your players are and how advanced their baseball skills are. See how newcomers might mesh—or not—with the boys from your current team.

Be up front with the parents and the players so they're fully aware of what they're getting themselves into. They deserve to know your practice and game schedules, all the costs, and especially what's expected of them. This is the time to talk about the importance of character studies and how they will be implemented. Paint as real a picture as possible of your current team, including your expectations, to see if a new player will be the right fit. The youth experience is too short to be miserable for even one season. The boys deserve better than that. Do your homework, because one disgruntled family can ruin everything.

Get-Good vs. Feel-Good Work

At the major-league level, we had several hours a day, every day, to help players hone their skills. But even they don't improve as much during the season as they do during the offseason. In the big leagues, the manager and the coaches' job is to prepare guys to compete every night, so initiating wholesale changes over the course of a season is difficult.

One of the coaches I had on my staff, Alec Zumwalt, referred to two different kinds of work: he said there was "Get-Good Work," which helped a player get better, and there was "Feel-Good Work," which simply made him feel better about himself. Both of those are important outcomes, but it should be obvious that one is much more valuable than the other.

Unfortunately, for decades the majority of the work we did during the major-league season was "Feel-Good Work," which built the confidence of the player and put him in a peak mental state to compete against the best talent in the world. Feel-Good work might involve taking batting practice off a pitcher exactly 45 feet away (as opposed to the regulation 60 feet, 6 inches), throwing exactly 52 mph and right down the middle of the plate. Contrast that with what a hitter faces over the course of a game: an elite pitcher throwing nasty fastballs, sometimes over 100 mph and flirting with the corners of the plate. And soon the starter is replaced, often by someone bigger, stronger, and even harder-throwing, specializing in giving 100 percent over just one or two innings.

The Feel-Good workout goal for the player then is designed to simply give him a feel for his swing and build that muscle memory of driving shots all over the yard. His likelihood of success during that workout is high because so many variables are controlled.

Similar Feel-Good work is designed for catching groundballs, flyballs, and even pitching in the bullpen. The player is not testing his limits but rather is getting in repetitions that give him confidence. As I say, Feel-Good work has its place. Players need a healthy dose of self-assurance. But there also must be a balance of challenge, a dose of stress, and frankly, failure. I happen to be a proponent of actually practicing pressure—incorporating stressors to force improvement and prepare a player for the pressure of the actual game. Baseball, like life, offers the greatest opportunity for growth after failure.

So how do you move from Feel-Good work to Get-Good work? You add to or take away some of the variables. I have seen special glasses for fielders that limit peripheral vision so they have to focus solely on the flight of the ball. Needless to say, you'd want to be careful with such a tool for younger players. There are also reaction balls that bounce in unexpected directions, giving players experience with bad hops.

The variables are limitless on the hitting side. You can change the distance between the pitcher and the hitter, increase the speed of the pitch, decrease the size and weight of the ball, increase the length and weight of the bat, you name it. You can even tinker with the amount of light or the color of the backdrop.

Admittedly, there is a fine line to walk between how much failure should actually occur before you risk the kids' psyches with too many negative results. You don't want mechanical flaws to set in due to mental or physical fatigue. If you're coaching the youngest (6–8 year-olds), beginning players, I would not recommend implementing *any* such stress variables.

Indoor Practices

At times you may be forced to practice indoors. Here's a quick list of what you can do inside in a confined space:

Indoor Practice Rotation

- Chalk talk with the magnetic whiteboard

- Stretching
- Everyone playing catch
- Pitching and catching (while their arms are loose)
- Defensive circuit
- Hitting circuit
- Character studies

Indoor practices will vary, depending on the type of space you have. Maximizing reps is the goal once again, while keeping the boys active. As much as you can, follow the model of the outdoor batting-practice stations. Be creative with different styles of balls and bats. Long toss may be a challenge but can be simulated against netting. Outfielders will be limited on what they can work on, but many barehand drills and first-step reaction drills can be performed indoors.

Fun

As I've said, especially for players 6–10 years old, the focus should be on fun and learning, and too much failure could result in their losing interest in the game. That's why you want to make every drill enjoyable. Give your youngest players the highest chance of success by increasing the size of the ball and the bat whenever possible. The QR code at left links to a video of me playing Big Ball with my two oldest grandsons.

Big Ball

I played this game with my own kids early on, and it took on a life of its own. I use a large bouncy ball and give them a Bamm-Bamm-sized bat (remember *The Flintstones*?) to virtually guarantee their odds of contact. We progressed from there to a version of kickball with a bat and ball and however many bases we had the space for. This can be played with as few as four kids, one base, and home plate. When they hit the ball they can be forced out or "pegged" with the ball before they get to the base near the pitcher's mound, or they can score. They loved it because all of them could hit a giant bouncing ball, and they could also catch and throw that ball without special skills. They had fun without even realizing that their baseball skills were improving.

Avoiding Failure

If you want to see a child walk away from baseball, do one of two things: let them fail often, or have them fear pain. Of course none of us wants that, so as you prepare for your practices, I would advise prioritizing fun. If it's not fun, all the emphasis on repetition and instruction becomes moot anyway.

Fun comes from success and competition. At the major-league level, managers and coaches capitalize on and exploit the natural competitiveness of players. We turned every drill—some of which might have otherwise become boring—into a competition with themselves and or against each other. Guess what? That means there will be winners and losers, another way to prepare them for the fact that not everyone gets a trophy at the end of the season. A worthy challenge for you is to design drills that allow every kid a chance to occasionally be a winner.

Be creative and pair the most athletic boys with those who have lesser natural ability. That way they will likely be part of the winning side in a friendly drill competition. Be careful not to allow anyone to show animosity toward or disappointment with those who don't perform as well as the others. They'll be encouraged when their team wins. This will go hand in hand with the character studies you're walking them through.

The Will to Win vs. Winning at All Costs

I believe people are built to compete and maximize the gifts they've been given. During my professional career, I constantly challenged my guys to make the most of the opportunities they enjoyed so that at the end of a day, a season, or a career, they could be proud and have no regrets.

The will to win is what should make a person approach life without taking one day for granted. But therein lies the danger I've warned you about since page one: adults forcing this mindset onto kids who just want to have fun. While a competitive spirit and the will to win are planted early and can be nurtured through time, losses during those early years actually create more teachable moments than victories.

So my recommendation? When you're not playing games established within your own youth league, schedule games against teams very similar to yours, but also schedule games against teams that will almost certainly badly beat you. You'll be amazed at how the kids respond to those losses. They will immediately see that there are kids out there, their own age and likely their own size, much better than they are. They'll learn they have much to work on, both individually and as a team.

Don't misunderstand me. Just because more can be learned through failure than success doesn't mean you want them losing every game. Constant failure results in its own issues. Just be sure that you and their parents don't overreact to the losses. If you don't overreact, the kids won't either. We're talking about kids just starting a sport, so their outlook will obviously change over time. But the lessons they learn early will stay with them.

Be sure to schedule games late in the season with the same teams that beat them early. If your kids have worked, honed their skills, and developed character, the games should be closer now.

Resist the temptation that too many coaches yield to—entering leagues or tournaments they feel they can dominate, just so they can tell the world about their championships. Some of that kind of success can be positive, but beating up every team you play will not push these kids to work hard on their weaknesses.

I know this goes against the grain. I want to win every endeavor I enter, and most likely you do too. The problem is that in order to create an atmosphere for a young person to reach their true potential, they must first develop a love and a passion for their sport. Before any other lessons can be taught, including the will to win, this atmosphere must be created.

Argue with me all you want, but I've had this borne out by players I've coached, men who coached me, and even former teammates. I'm grateful for people who challenge my thinking on many issues, like this one.

An Important Caveat

Resist the temptation to arbitrarily assign each player to a specific position. Sure, you want to know where they see themselves playing and what position they prefer, so maybe that's where you start them in the following drills. But it's vitally important for several reasons to rotate every player through every position, not just in drills and practices, but also in games. With the possible exception of kids who, for whatever reason, have no interest in playing behind the plate, everybody should learn every position, practice it, and try it in a real game.

Why?

Not just because they might surprise themselves with how much they like a position they hadn't considered before, but also because they need to know and understand what their teammates face when they play that position. That's one of the reasons every player should learn to pitch and get some experience on the mound. It's easy to be critical of a teammate when he can't seem to find the plate or get anyone out—until you've spent an inning or more in his shoes.

With every eye in the ballpark on you, from the umpires to your parents to everyone else's parents, to your teammates on the field and on the bench, to the batter, the guy on deck, and the entire opposing team—how are you doing now? Maybe you *wanted* to pitch, to be the guy, to show off your control, your fastball, your strategy. Then your first pitch is high and wide. The next almost hits the batter. The third is in the dirt.

You know you're better than this, but with every pitch, the pressure and tension grow. You hear the groans, see the grimaces, and are desperate to find your groove and prove what you can do. Let me tell you, even if you never pitch again, you'll never forget that pressure and what it takes to perform with all those eyes on you. Bottom line, at the very least it will make you a better teammate.

By the same token, kids who are scared to death to pitch and just know they have nothing to offer will sometimes surprise themselves with how they do. Even if their pitches are miles per hour slower than others', they may find that this throws off the other team. All of a sudden your player likes this pitching thing and wants to try it again.

While that's magnified on the pitching rubber, it's also true for every other position. Players who like the idea of, in essence, quarterbacking the team as the catcher quickly face a rude awakening when a foul tip hits the face mask and rings their bell. Or when a wild pitch slams an exposed inner thigh or even a cup-protected crotch. How fun is it now to think about what pitch to signal the pitcher to throw?

Does first base look easy? All you have to do is catch the ball and step on the bag, right? What about those short-hop throws that the big leaguers make look so easy? What happens when one sneaks under your glove? You're not wearing shin guards like the catcher, and you could take that ball anywhere. That's a position where you won't forget your cup a second time.

A wrong first step in the outfield can mean the difference between a routine catch of a flyball or a triple that goes all the way to the wall. And what about the adrenaline that makes a kid not only miss the cutoff man but also send the ball soaring all the way to the backstop?

All that is to say there are dangers and unknowns at every position that you won't fully understand unless you've played there. Pitchers need experience in every other position too. That will cure them of slumping their shoulders or shaking their heads when a teammate misplays a ball or throws to the wrong base. It's all about empathy. Knowing the conventions and expectations and all the things that can go wrong at every position will quickly turn a kid into an encourager instead of a critic.

So, while you may assign kids to specific position drills at first, make sure everybody takes his turn at every position. The videos I link to for each drill will be revised and updated as necessary, so click on them regularly to see the latest version.

All You Need

Throughout this book you'll find QR links with video instructions for how coaches should conduct infield practice, hit flyballs to the outfielders, and coach from first and third base. Hitting groundballs, flyballs, and pop-ups looks easy when big-league coaches are doing it. But it takes practice and lots of

Fungo Bats and Tennis Rackets

Fungo Technique

Improving at Home

repetition. Not every assistant coach will be confident he can do this. If you know how, you can try to show them, but it's also okay to do this with a tennis racket instead of a regular or fungo bat. More on fungo bats and tennis rackets here. You'll get a lot more natural control as you learn how the ball flies off the strings.

One of the very young players I coached was challenged to improve his fielding. He really enjoyed throwing the ball off a brick wall and fielding it both barehanded and with a glove. I was amazed at his desire and discipline of doing this drill, and the results were equally astounding. While he was working on his hand-eye coordination and proficiency with his glove, he was also getting throwing repetitions and working on his accuracy, without even knowing it. Here he is now, as a player in the Colorado Rockies organization, explaining those drills he undertook as a youngster.

No Standing Around

I'm a stickler about a lot of elements of a good practice session, but one thing I'm absolutely adamant about is this: No one should ever be standing around with nothing to do. No one. If they're standing around, you soon lose them. So have every drill and activity scheduled to the minute and make sure you and your assistants are enforcing that rule—even synchronizing your watches. I know that sounds militant, but it's necessary to keep from having groups lagging when it's time to move the players to different drills. Your kids may not face the same ultimatums that big leaguers do, where they have to perform every minute or lose their lifelong dream, but there's no excuse for them to stand idle.

Ideally you want three or four players in each group so each player gets the maximum number of repetitions for whatever it is you're teaching that day. Even your youngest players, whether they realize it or not, crave structure. It takes a lot of work to be prepared for every minute of a practice session, but it's worth the effort.

What Stuck with Players

"There was always something to do. You were either picking up stray balls or hitting off a tee while waiting to hit in the cage. Or you might be fielding, running, soft-tossing. A lot of us were used to just hanging with our friends and maybe getting in some batting practice. That wasn't the goal here. We were to get better each week in the short time we had. It wasn't that it couldn't be fun but that you were going to have fun *because* you were getting better and not standing still."

Repetitions

If there is one differentiator for young athletes in any sport developing their skills, it would absolutely be repetitions. The boys you coach who will develop the most and improve the fastest will be those who simply love grabbing a ball and figuring out fun things to do with it. They don't even consider it practice or work.

If you expect to see these young men improve their baseball skills in only your hour- or hour-and-a-half-long practice, you might see minimal gains. I tell parents and players alike that real improvement comes from the work they do aside from organized practice. Most parents and players will need guidance as to what they can do at home together and what the player can do at home alone. But you'll find that kids who really love the game enjoy playing it anywhere and everywhere. Offer them the hints from upcoming chapters about how to do their repetitions at home—throwing, fielding, running, and hitting—and watch them flourish.

7

The Nuts and Bolts

Part 1: The Warm-up

All right, so here we are, at a point where the real work begins. I could have titled this Teaching Kids the Game. It will stretch over two chapters, because my goal is to give you a detailed road map of how to conduct practices and train your players.

A Practice Plan

By now I hope you're desperate for a basic, fundamental, easy-to-follow list of exactly how to run a practice. Well, here you go. I'll explain how I organized and prioritized outdoor practices at the major-league level and how that same format can translate to your practice time.

One obvious difference between your youth-league workouts and the spring training ones I conducted in Florida for the Cardinals and in Arizona for the Royals is that I was not restricted by the clock. I am guessing your field, gym, or cage space will be limited to an hour, and even that might be pushing the attention span of your young players, especially the 6–9 year-olds. The 10–12 year-olds may be able to focus a little longer, but not much.

There was a method to the madness of my practice structure for spring training, but your practice can be run similarly. Big leaguers are physically and mentally able to handle more repetitions, and we had multiple fields to maximize our time, but the sequence and content of the drills will be the same.

The league you're in will determine your playing schedule, but you will determine how much practice to try to work in each week. I recommend at least one full hour practice per week for the younger ages and 90 minutes for the 10–12 year-olds. With that limited schedule it becomes even more important that you establish one specific priority for each workout and attack that skill as soon as the boys are loose and still somewhat focused.

For the 10–12 year-olds, the warm-up portion need take no more than 30 minutes and can be completed in 20 if you're pressed for time.

As you work your way through the sequences I suggest below, keep in mind that one key to accomplishing a short but effective warm-up is keeping the attention of the boys and not allowing it to become merely socializing time. You can also compress base-running drills by establishing that once one of the boys is halfway to the next base, the following boy should be going.

Playing catch may seem like a leisurely activity, but in reality it should be one of the most serious parts of practice. Remind the players that this isn't messing-around time, but rather when they should be perfecting the art of throwing to targets and catching properly. People often mention how effortless big leaguers make these elements look. You can bet it's because they took it seriously from day one.

Then, team fundamentals can be completed in 15 minutes, and individual defensive drills can be done during batting practice—which can be completed in 45 minutes, even while working in many at-bat repetitions and hitting groundballs and flyballs to defenders.

Some days you might want to focus an entire practice session on one of the aforementioned skills.

I structured our day in two parts, in the following order:

- **Warm-up:** Stretching, Baserunning, Playing Catch
- **Skills:** Team Fundamentals, Individual Defense Drills, Batting Practice

Activity 1: Stretching

We always limbered up first, something that has been practiced for centuries. You will have slightly different stretches for 6–8 year-olds as opposed to 9–10 year-olds and 11–12 year-olds. The video linked at right shows how to perform static stretching (sitting or standing), as well as active stretches—which I prefer to keep the boys moving and not messing around (the same was true for my big leaguers).

Stretching

Activity 2: Baserunning

Right after stretching you want to take advantage of their loose legs and get a little more of their pent-up energy out of them. Baseball is not a cardiovascular sport, but a little distance running is good for endurance and overall health. Just don't overdo it. Baseball training should employ more of an interval method—bursts of speed and effort, and then rest.

One efficient way to incorporate it into your practice plan is to conduct some basic baserunning drills. I suggest starting every practice with the sequence below. Major-league guys do some variation of it almost daily through spring training, and it's often reviewed throughout the regular season. I also suggest that you take a video of the first day of trying these drills, and then video them at the end of the season. You'll be amazed at the improvement in your players and also in your coaches.

These drills obviously take up some of your precious field time, but you can always do the stretching and baserunning drills prior to your allotted field time if you can find open space. Portable bases that won't slide out from under their feet are handy for makeshift drills.

Drill 1: Home to First Base

Have the boys take a fake swing in the batter's box and run through first base. You rarely want to assign one-at-a-time repetitions with large groups, because it is an inefficient use of your time and the boys will get bored. But baserunning is an exception because it's important to closely watch their form when touching the base and running through the bag. Admittedly, baserunning for the youngest ages might start with just letting them know which base to run to.

The most important tip when running to first base on a ball hit to the infield is to focus on the base and not watch the ball. Next most important is to hit the front of the bag with the ball of either foot while leaning forward. The legendary base stealer Maury Wills always emphasized, "*Through* the bag, not *to* the bag." Make a mark five feet past the base and have them run through the mark after touching the front of first base with either foot. Finally, teach them that once they hit the bag they should look over their right shoulder for an errant throw they might advance on, while also listening to the coach, who will be shouting in-

Home to First

structions. The QR code on the previous page links to a video that explains this in more detail.

Your first-base coach should be shouting, "Hard through the base, through the base, through the base!" If a ball gets past the first baseman, the coach should swing his left arm, yelling, "Go, go, go!" while pointing toward second with his right. If the ball gets past the first baseman by only a little, the coach can say, "Stay here, stay here, stay here!" while pointing at first base. I'm not sure where the idea of repeating three times came from, but it has worked in the big leagues for a long time, so it's a good practice to copy. During practice is a great time for the coaches to get repetitions at this. No hand signals will be needed from the first-base coach when the runner is just running through the bag. Try to get each kid two or three repetitions of running out of the box through first base.

Drill 2: Home to Second Base

Your next baserunning drill should be from home to second base on a double. The boys should individually take a swing (without a bat) and visualize a ball going through the infield. Instruct them to pick up the first-base coach and begin the proper turn around first base. The video linked at right clarifies this.

Home to Second

This is also a great chance for your first-base coach to begin working on his responsibilities. He can mix things up for each boy, deciding to either round him to second (as discussed above) or to pretend that the outfielder has gotten to the ball quickly and shout, "Round and stay!" three times.

Something your boys can graduate to would be the coach shouting, "Round and look!" three times, allowing them to decide for themselves whether they should keep going after they hit the base. It's fun to watch young players start to make decisions for themselves, but they need to practice hearing these instructions and physical cues.

The technique for touching first base on a turn is a little more complicated than running through, and often even professional players don't get it right. The most time-efficient turn at first base has the player hit the front inside corner with their right foot. This can be difficult for kids to grasp at the early ages and may result in some stutter stepping or stumbling, but it's worth working on. Have your first-base coach watch their footing and praise them, even if they only accidentally hit the bag with the correct foot. The reason for the right-foot turn and the technique is shown in the above video. After a couple of reps of home to second, have the boys go to first base.

Right Foot Tag on Bases

Drill 3: First to Third Base

Now you'll work on the boys going from first to third. Again, this is a great opportunity for your first- and third-base coaches to become familiar with properly signaling the boys with physical and verbal instructions. Have the kids start either on the bag or with a lead (depending on your league rules), and then have them visualize a groundball through the infield to the outfield. The first-base coach will shout, "Go, go, go!" and the player should begin his footwork on the way to second that sets him up for a turn toward third base. You might even set up some simple cones or even plastic cups to indicate the proper angle toward second, as demonstrated in the video linked just above.

First to Third

As soon as the ball gets past the infield, the baserunner should pick up the third-base coach, whose physical signals will be even more important than the verbal because of the distance. A wave of the left arm tells the runner to keep coming all the way to third. Have another coach watch that the bag is touched at second, preferably with the right foot on the inside corner for efficiency of movement.

Occasionally, perhaps every fourth or fifth runner, the third-base coach should throw up the stop sign, raising both arms and moving toward the runner. He can shout, "Stop, stop, stop!" or "Back, back, back!" if they have already made the turn to third and are at risk of being thrown out at second.

I don't suggest your players sliding into third every time you do this drill, but occasionally is not a bad idea. Most times, the third-base coach should have his left hand in the air and right index finger pointing at the bag, saying "Up, up, up!" if there is no play. If there *would* be a play on them, the coach should wave both arms toward the bag and shout, "Down, down, down!" indicating that the boy should slide. For more on sliding technique and strategy, see the video.

Sliding

The last option is the coach moving down the baseline toward home while waving his left arm, indicating the baserunner should keep coming, prepare for a right-foot tag of the base, and watch the coach. This is the most challenging baserunning play your coach will have at third, allowing the play to develop before deciding to throw up the stop sign at the last instant or send him to the plate. Both arms in the air and yelling, "Stop, stop, stop!" "Back, back, back!" or windmilling one arm and shouting, "Go, go, go!"

Then have the boys jog to first and do this first-to-third drill at least a couple of times.

Drill 4: Second Base to Third Base/Home

Next have them go to second base and prepare for a ball that gets through the infield. The third-base coach becomes critically important again, as the ball will be behind the runner and he will have to rely solely on the coach. As soon as the ball is hit, the coach should make his way toward home, and the runner will begin his turn at third toward home (again, cones or cups can help determine the proper line). The coach will swing his left arm for the runner to advance or throw up the stop sign. Watch major-league third-base coaches to see how animated they can be. They might be shouting too, but most of the time they can't be heard because of the crowd noise, so physical signals are crucial. Work on having the boys both try to score and scamper back to third. On a groundball hit to third or shortstop, the runner should hold, even with two outs, to force the fielder to throw to first. See the video linked above showing this.

Second to Home

Drill 5: Third Base to Home

Finally, have the boys start at third base. The third-base coach will instruct them to tag up on a flyball with fewer than two outs. Have each boy move down the line a couple of steps for their secondary lead (see the video linked at left). As they visualize the flyball being hit, the third-base coach should holler, "Tag, tag, tag!" The runner should return to third and tag up with their left foot on the base so they're facing the outfield and can see when the ball is caught. (The only time they would tag with their right

Third to Home

foot is on a foul ball down the third base/left field line so they're facing the fielder in foul territory. That can be complicated for younger players, but it's fun to challenge them to learn it.)

Once you've visualized the ball being caught in the outfield, the third-base coach shouts, "Go, go, go!" and you teach the runner to run hard through home plate, like they would at first base. Older players can be taught the importance of crossing the plate before a potential third out can be made on another player, which would nullify the run.

An advanced version of this drill has a player who has already scored or is waiting to hit to stand at least ten feet beyond home plate and signal the runner to stay up or slide, using the same hand signals the third-base coach uses. This increases the odds of your baserunner scoring and can also keep him from getting hurt. Consider having your young players always slide into home plate, because often his teammate won't know if there will be a play. It's always safer to slide than to risk an accidental collision with the catcher.

Do the third-base tag-up drill a couple of times, and by now the boys should be properly loosened up and a little tired.

Activity 3: Throwing and Catching

The time your players spend just playing catch each day can be one of the most important elements of the practice. Too often, players of all ages miss the importance of this and mess around during catch time. I know fun will always be the most important goal, but learning proper skills and techniques will be a close second. Playing catch can teach so many good or potentially bad habits.

I often asked my catchers how many balls they threw a day. Most couldn't come up with a number. But when you take into account just playing catch, then long-tossing with the starting pitcher, then 150 or more pitches per game (most of which they'll throw back to the pitcher), plus the warm-up pitches between every inning and the throw to second base between innings—it's a lot of throws.

I then ask them how many of those throws are focused on technique and accuracy. Usually the answer is, "Not many."

The fact is, players reinforce habits with every throw—good ones or bad ones. Baseball is all about throwing to targets. First, take a few minutes to give young arms a quick stretch. The first video shows a couple of stretches they can do before their playing catch session. Then, be sure your players take the five or so minutes of catch time seriously and work on something specific. A catcher may work on proper arm motion, or on the exchange between the glove and the hand. Other players should work on the four-seam grip, which I demonstrate in the second video. But all players should work on hitting a target while playing catch. Award points for each target hit, and the kids can keep a running total against each other. That's a fun way to add some friendly competition to playing catch.

At the earliest ages, tell players they are not allowed to throw a ball during catch unless their partner is holding up a target. This accomplishes two things: 1) it helps them practice getting a ball to a specific point, and 2) it keeps a younger player from getting hit with a ball he might not know was coming. The third video shows a sequence of arm-loosening catch drills I used through most of my career.

Arm Stretches

Seam Grips

Arm-Loosening Drills

After the catch-playing sequence is done and the arms are loose, this is a great time to stretch it out by playing long toss. That's just what it sounds like—throwing the ball as far as they can with relative accuracy. Don't let them get ridiculously too far from each other, but allow them to test their ability to make far, accurate throws.

Beginner Long Toss

At the professional levels, naturally, the guys tend to have a rhythm and snap to their throws that makes them fun to watch, even just playing catch. Eventually everybody at that level plays long toss where they really air it out. Pitchers and infielders will sometimes even do this in the outfield.

Advanced Long Toss

For the youngest ages, you can use soft balls with no gloves to develop eye-hand coordination. They can catch two-handed and have fun keeping track of how many catches they make in a row. Then they can progress to small, baseball-sized balls that are still soft and practice rolling the ball to each other until they're comfortable taking throws.

Beginner Long Toss Drills

For the 9–10 year-olds, emphasize the importance of the lead arm (the gloved hand) pointing at the target and aggressively pulling down to the glove-side hip on the throw—important for increased velocity, accuracy, and arm health. You always want them practicing the four-seam grip, because that grip makes the ball more predictable in flight. A beginner struggles to hold the ball with two fingers, but you'll want them to learn how as soon as they're big enough. A throw of a ball

Front Side

held with three or more fingers essentially becomes a change-up. So, for the truest, most accurate throw with the most velocity and carry, teach that two-finger release from a four-seam grip, demonstrated in the last video on the previous page.

For the older kids, start with them on their knees for more controlled tosses, then progress to one knee, stride foot forward (opposite of their throwing arm, of course) to increase intensity, and moving targets. Usually you want them throwing to the middle of the chest, feet shoulder-width apart, arm at a 90-degree angle, working the wrist forward, then back, then throwing. They should keep their stride foot forward beyond shoulder width and the transfer of weight from back foot to front foot.

Using Legs to Throw

Summary

Getting the body loose, running the bases, and playing catch every day can become either a bore or an opportunity to get better. That's why it's so important for you to impress on the kids the difference this training can make in their individual and team improvement.

Any athletic trainer will tell you how important flexibility and muscle warmth are to maximize performance and minimize potential injury.

Running the bases can feel like punishment in your players' minds unless you teach them to take pride in doing it properly. Teams that learn effective baserunning turn it into a potent weapon.

Playing catch can be the most productive time of your day if your players take the time and make the effort to throw properly, concentrate on hitting targets, and make a habit of stretching their arms out with effective long toss.

Big leaguers perform this exact routine for their entire careers, and the best ones appreciate a coach who holds them accountable to continue to get better.

8

The Nuts and Bolts

Part 2: The Skills

After your boys' arms and legs are loose, it's time to teach skills. Let's be honest, most of them are concerned only with batting practice, because it is fun at any age. So keep that carrot dangling in front of them until the end. If you find them not taking some of the other drills seriously enough, tell them their hitting time will be sacrificed until they get their other work done.

Activity 4: Team Fundamentals

At each practice, focus on one of the five fundamentals on the following page. If you're looking for something major to set you apart from typical youth-league coaches, it's the fundamentals. It's surprising how many miss the basics. Sure, we're all thrilled if we can find kids with hitting power or big arms, but it's the basic skills that win in the long run. That means knowing the game situation, how many outs there are, where the runners are, what base to throw to, how to keep the ball in front of you, and communicating with teammates—all while repeating the essentials on the following page.

1.
Cut Offs
and Relays

2.
Pop-up
Priority

3.
Bunt
Defense

4.
First and Third
Double Steals

5.
Rundowns

Keep the drills short: a couple of minutes to explain the drill and then five to ten minutes running it. Legendary manager Whitey Herzog always drilled the same team fundamental two practices in a row. The first day was more of a walk-through and the next was less talking and more repetitions. The first day you introduce a drill, you might want to show the kids what it looks like on the whiteboard.

Activity 5:
Individual Defense Practice

Because every player needs to know the basics of every position, assign groups of three or no more than four players to each defensive station. One coach should be assigned to each group or station.

Assuming you have a team of twelve players, you'll want three players working in the outfield, three in the infield, three pitchers pitching to screens (start close and emphasize the strike zone), and three players engaging in PFP (pitchers' fielding practice). Remember, these individual drills last only so long, and then everyone rotates to another station. So every player is experiencing every drill.

Drill 1: Groundballs

For 6–8 year-olds

Begin by rolling groundballs to the players from close proximity, whether they're infielders or outfielders. Progress to hitting soft rag balls to them. These are balls slightly larger than a baseball and softer than a softball. The kids should catch with two hands and throw to a coach or a screen and rotate after every rep.

Beginner Groundballs

Progress to balls to their left and then to their right, fielding with a glove and without a glove. For proper footwork training, watch this video.

You and your assistant coaches may struggle in hitting effective groundballs, so get in as many reps as possible by just rolling them. You might also find it easier to use a tennis racket and soft foam balls for hitting grounders and flyballs.

Infielder Feeds and Footwork

For 9–12 year-olds

Slightly older kids are ready for more advanced footwork to get around the ball and generate momentum for the throw to first base.

Advanced Groundballs

Turning Two

They should also be ready for more advanced feeds to second base—flips, backhands, underhands, and when to throw overhand—which are demonstrated in the videos linked above. You can even introduce instruction for footwork and tosses for turning a double play.

Catching groundballs is an art, and when it is done properly, it is beautiful to watch. Above are some groundball drills for proper positioning and technique to teach your young players.

Beginner Flyballs

Drill 2: Flyballs

For 6–8 year-olds

Check out this video for how to progress with beginners from bare two-handed catches of larger balls to one-handed catching with a glove. Insisting on two-handed catches has become archaic, and you'll notice that almost all big leaguers find it easier and more natural with one hand.

Advanced Flyballs

For 9–12 year-olds

Older kids are ready to learn the drop step, charging the ball, fielding outside the glove-side knee, and even the crow-hop throw.

Diving Catch **Outfield Drills**

You can also teach them how to properly dive for a ball (they love this).

Above, you'll also find other outfield drills.

Drill 3: Pitching Practice

You know I advise that everyone get a chance to pitch, but I would go further and suggest that you tell each kid that the team *needs* him to pitch. That way no one gets overworked or hurts their arm. Here's an orthopedic doctor speaking on this.

Orthopedic Advice

Lesser-talented kids often shy away from pitching because it's such a high-pressure and visible position. But once you get them out there and they throw a few strikes and eventually get some outs, they feel like they're a big part of the team. When they see they can do it, they start working harder on their throwing and become better overall players.

Admittedly, with 6–8 year-olds, they're just standing at the pitcher position and learning to field, because their opponents are either hitting off a tee or their coach is pitching to them. That's to keep from having an endless game of walks or pitches hitting the backstop. During practices you can still have a pitching drill, but basically you're just trying to get them to throw a strike. Some eight-year-olds are starting kid pitch, and in that case a coach might take over after three walks in an inning.

For 9–10 year-olds, kid pitching usually begins. Don't make it too complicated for them. Rather just have them think of the plate in halves and have their catchers calling for inside or outside pitches, setting up on the inner or outer half of the plate.

I recommend only two-seam and four-seam fastballs and change-ups even through twelve years old. No breaking-ball spin pitches. Leave that to their next coach. But even more important than avoiding curves and sliders at this age is simple overuse, as mentioned above. Here's a video with multiple change-up grips you can teach your pitchers.

Catcher Setup

For your pitchers to get their repetitions, you might need to add a station in the defensive drills circuit so three boys can pitch. This also gives your catchers repetitions behind the plate, but they need to get some reps on the mound as well. Sometimes you'll have more pitchers than catchers, but you can use nets with strike zones to serve as the catcher. I prefer the ones that display a nine-box grid, separating the strike zone into three boxes each for away, middle, and inside vertically, and top of the zone, middle of the zone, and bottom of the zone horizontally. As the boys progress, they should be aiming for one of those nine sections with every throw.

Change-up Grips

Box Strike Zone

Then there is the matter of how many pitches a kid needs to throw before coming into a game, along with what else they need to accomplish while warming up. Little League Baseball recommends the following:

Ages 7–8: 50 pitches per day
Ages 9–10: 75 pitches per day
Ages 11–12: 85 pitches per day

This video includes more pitching drills and philosophies.

Pitching Drills

Drill 4: PFP (Pitchers' Fielding Practice)

Run your pitchers through covering first base on a ball hit to the first baseman. Each player can rotate from pitcher to first baseman and then get back in line.

Each should field grounders back to the mound and throw to first. Then, because your infielders are also on the field, pitchers can field grounders and throw to second. All should take groundballs at all infield positions, even lefties.

PFP Rotation

What Stuck with Players

"When I first found out about rotating positions, I was ecstatic. I'd been pigeonholed as a short middle infielder, when the fact was that I'd always dreamed of being Albert Pujols at first base or even Coach Matheny behind the plate. Rotating was a blast. We got to see and learn the game from perspectives we may never have had before. We had to learn outfield positioning and relays, even if we had only ever played infield."

PFP Explained

Drill 5: Fielding from the Mound

Check out this video to teach pitchers how to handle:

- Come-backers to throw to first base
- Come-backers to throw to second base
- Covering first
- Communication between first baseman and pitcher on balls hit between them
- Covering first base on 3-6-1 double play
- Developing the habit of getting to first base when any ball is hit to the right side. The catcher and you should be shouting, "Get over!" every time.

Drill 6: Catching Practice

It is very hard to teach catching unless you know what you are looking for. As a Dad Coach, you can learn much from instructional videos. See the links on the following pages for some great catching drills.

This is the one position that can be the exception to the every-position rule. Many kids are just afraid to get back there, and I would absolutely not make them try it. But for the ones who are eager or at least willing to try it, catching can change a life. It changed mine. Catchers have been called the quarterbacks of baseball, which I get because not only was I a catcher for my entire playing life, but I was also a high school football quarterback. Players at both positions are expected to call the plays. While the pitcher may necessarily and understandably be the focal point, the catcher runs the show on the field.

That's a lot of fun and a heavy responsibility, but it's also a lot of work—not only for your catchers, but for you as a coach. It's arguably the hardest position to coach because of its importance. It's widely accepted in baseball that poor play behind the plate can cost you more runs than poor play at any other position besides pitching.

After a career as a catcher, imagine how blessed I felt as a manager to get to coach both Yadier (Yadi) Molina with the St. Louis Cardinals and Salvador (Salvy) Pérez with the Kansas City Royals. I can't imagine the pain felt by managers who didn't have such superstars behind the plate so deftly handling the many demands.

So, what do you look for in a catcher?

1. **Conscientiousness:** This may surprise you, but I prioritize conscientiousness the most because it's the characteristic that makes a player the most teachable. (More on this on the following page.)
2. **Catching pitches:** This sounds like a no-brainer, but stay with me. It is what the position is all about, but there's so much more than you might think to catching a pitch. You don't want catchers stabbing at the ball, and there's much to learn about gathering the ball in, framing it for the umpire, and how and where to catch a pitch when you're planning to throw out a runner.

Pitch Framing

3 (tie). **Controlling the running game with a strong, accurate throwing arm** and **Blocking balls in the dirt:** Both are dependent on a pitcher doing his part.

Catchers Footwork and Blocking

4. **Effectively calling a game:** This one might also surprise you, but this is the age when you can start teaching catchers a game plan, how to call pitches, and to have a "why" for every pitch they call. They are more capable of doing this than we give them credit for. I am a firm believer in having catchers call the pitches from as early an age as they can manage it. Sure, they'll make mistakes and will have to learn a lot of things the hard way like I did, but it makes no sense to have the catcher looking into the dugout for the coach's signal for pitches. Of course I'm speaking as a former catcher, but I suffered through one college year of my coach calling all the pitches, and I was greatly relieved when Bill Freehan became my coach and insisted I call the game—as I had done from youth league all the way up through high school. That's how it should be done.

Pitch Calling

More on Conscientiousness and Catching

A catcher must possess the heart and, yes, even the desire to take foul balls off their arms, legs, and not-so-fun other places, while celebrating a ball that hits him in the chest after it bounces in the dirt. A friend of mine happened to be in a big-league locker room while the players were dressing before a game and was stunned to see that the everyday catcher was literally bruised head to toe wherever he didn't have protective gear—arms, shoulders, thighs, and backs of legs. Both hands looked like every finger had been broken and taped back together.

Yet there are guys—and I was one of them—who didn't want

to play anywhere else. If a player is wired for this position, it's simply hard for them to play anywhere else. I was asked a few times to finish a game at first base so our famed slugger Mark McGwire could get a few innings off his feet. Like any other player, I'd do anything for the team and was glad to, but I found it hard to not be involved with every pitch.

Behind the plate I loved the constant dance with the pitcher, using verbal and physical signs to help them survive and thrive. The constant demand of calling pitches and guiding a pitching staff through a game, the thrill of cutting down a potential base thief, and serving as the quarterback on the field when it all hit the fan and other players are looking to you for decisions in real time—well, there's nothing like it.

Then there's the excitement of a play at the plate: fielding pop-ups, defending against bunts, double steals, and helping your coaches and manager interact with the umpire. What a great position! Of course, I'm biased, but just an aside from a proud catcher: don't let anyone refer to catcher's gear as the tools of ignorance. Ignorant players will not succeed as catchers. Rather, refer to their gear as the tools of intelligence. (That may be why a lot of big-league managers are former catchers.) Truth be told, there is no other position on the field with more responsibility and reward.

I will never forget the question my dad asked me when I was ten. I had been wearing him and my brother out begging to play baseball. He asked me, "Do you really want to be a good baseball player and play as long as you can?"

"Yes, sir!"

His response proved prophetic. "If you want to make the most of your talent, catching is the best and easiest way to play as long as you can."

Well, I learned it wasn't exactly the *easiest* part, as the position is grueling to master. But it was the *surest* way to succeed if you managed that. Catching certainly brought me many more opportunities than any other position would have. I would never had made the major leagues if I had not followed my father's advice.

I was incredibly fortunate that a coach named Ron Golden asked me to play on his team not long after that life-changing conversation with my dad. Not only was Golden the most advanced youth-level coach in the area, but he was also a former minor-league catcher in the Giants organization. Most impressive about Golden as I look back on it now is how hard it must have been for him to allow me to catch when his own son Eric was also a fine catcher.

There's a great lesson for all of us Dad Coaches. He absolutely could have nudged me toward another position, but he had the humility to be an honest evaluator of skills and potential, regardless of how it affected his son. (It turns out that Eric was one of the best youth-league infielders I had ever seen, and he went on to have a great career at the University of Central Florida as a second baseman.)

I'll always be grateful for my dad's wisdom in leading me down the path of least resistance—and the most bruises. He relentlessly encouraged me and never said no when I asked to play catch or work on my drills in the backyard. Ron Golden was light-years ahead of coaches in the art of catching. He beat me up with balls in the dirt and also allowed me to stumble through calling games. He would second-guess every pitch I called, and that gave me a strong "why" for the hundreds of thousands of pitches I would call in my career.

He also wasn't afraid to put me on the bench when I wasn't playing well and another player deserved the time. That taught me to grind, to fight, and to take pride in the most unique position on the field. I am forever grateful to be a part of the unique fraternity of catchers.

Check out the catching video for:

- How to give signs with nobody on base
- How to give signs with man on second base (multiple signs)
- A warm-up plan

Catcher Signs and Drills

Drill 7: Infield Practice

Here's another possible rotation that will give your players more infield repetitions:

For younger players, I suggest having at least three Dad Coaches (preferably four) available. You'll need one rolling groundballs to a group of three players at third base, one doing the same for three players at shortstop, and another for three boys at first base. (You'll see below when to work second base into the mix.) Your fourth group will be three players in the outfield, and you can rotate groups from the outfield to third, then to short, then to first. Keep the repetitions high, so no one's standing around.

At third base, start close and have the boys field the ball with their bare hands on the ground and practice their footwork for throwing to first base (without actually throwing). After a couple of repetitions, have them wear their gloves but still not throw.

After the first basemen have finished their barehand and glove drills, they will be ready to receive throws from across the infield. I suggest still rolling the balls at the early ages, for the purpose of repetitions. For older teams, use a fungo bat (here again is the video about that).

Advanced Fungos

See how many repetitions you can get over five minutes and then rotate.

At first base, get the boys prepared to take throws from across the third basemen by starting them positioned off the base and then running to the bag to take a few throws tosses from you barehanded, then with the glove, while working on proper footwork. Here is a video of the footwork for a first baseman getting to the base and tagging it properly, as well as other first-base drills. If you have time, you can simulate a few short hop throws in the dirt for first basemen to practice picking.

First-Base Drills

At shortstop, start with no glove again, and have the boys work on the proper footwork toward second base, without throwing. Add the glove for a few repetitions. You might tell them that major-league infielders conduct barehand drills almost every day, so this is anything but wasted time. Here is a video on groundball fielding technique and other drills.

More Infield Drills

After they field with the glove, rotate the boys from fielder to catching the ball at second base, then return to shortstop to field another groundball. Work on accurate throws, chest-high, and using the leg opposite their glove hand to stay on the base, like a first baseman. Alternate to second base in your next practice to work on fielding and throwing to the shortstop at second base from the second-base position.

Drill 8: Outfield Practice

Get in as many flyball repetitions as possible. As with the other positions, start barehanded and then add the glove. Then have the boys working on catching the ball while running and also charging a groundball. You will probably have time to work on only one skill per practice, but keep it fun by having them compete with each other when possible. Here are a few videos of techniques big leaguers use for catching a flyball, along with other drills to keep the boys challenged.

Outfield Drills

On Right Field

Have you ever noticed that the worst player on most youth-league teams gets dumped into right field? In the majors, you want a great fielder with a big arm out there. But in kids' ball, since the pitching is slower, most of the hitters are right-handed, and everyone seems to pull the ball, very few hits reach right field. But if you keep putting the same kid in right field for that reason, you risk their losing interest in the game altogether. Again, remember your overall purpose: fun, learning, and building character. Ideally you want these kids—not just your best players—to fall in love with the game.

Activity 6: Batting Practice

When it's finally time for this favorite drill, you have all kinds of options for all ages. You can start with golf-ball-sized Wiffle ball pitches, hitting off a tee into a net (though this may sound like a regression back to the lowest level of baseball, remember that even big leaguers often practice off a tee), overhand soft toss in a cage or on the field using limited-flight balls, or regular batting practice on the field with regulation baseballs so everyone can watch the flight and the carry. Above all, keep it fun. This is the highlight of the day for the guys. The trick is how to get as many swings as possible with your limited time and space.

I suggest small groups spread out over the field with different types of balls. Ideally, you want access to an outdoor batting cage, the best space for hitting real baseballs. The kids need to feel the resistance of the hardball coming off the bat, but that's not nearly as important as repetitions and building confidence.

One concern with traditional hardball batting practice is the risk of someone getting hit on the field. Plus you will have one batter and eleven bored little guys on your hands. You'll get the most productive repetitions having groups rotate. Separate the field into four stations if you're fortunate enough to have three other Dad Coaches assisting you. Maybe one group is in the cage for traditional batting practice, another is in the right field corner doing underhand soft toss with plastic golf balls, another in the left field corner hitting hard balls off a batting tee into a net.

If you can afford three tees and three nets, you'll greatly increase the number of overall swings. The last group can be on the field, hitting in the batter's box with a coach throwing overhand with plastic/foam balls. These travel just as far as hard balls but don't hurt if they hit someone who isn't paying attention. You also won't need an L-screen for the pitcher's protection if you use the other style of balls.

Many different drills can keep the boys engaged, so get creative in keeping score, letting the boys compete during the drills. Here are videos of some of our favorite hitting drills.

Hitting Drills

Have the boys rotate from one station to the next. A good rule of thumb is to have the boys waiting for their turn refrain from swinging their bats.

I suggest rounds of fewer than ten repetitions each before switching hitters, keeping the other boys loose and engaged.

You're going to discover that there's an art to throwing batting practice or coach-pitching a game. It's simply not as straightforward as it might appear when you're watching major-league hitters workout in the cage before a game. Big leaguers can be the most fickle bunch I have ever been around. I can't count the number of times I had a player tell me he just didn't like the BP (batting practice) throws of a certain coach—sometimes me.

I was never a good enough hitter to complain about a coach's throwing skills, but I certainly had some who made batting practice tougher than others. The fact is, batting practice is Feel-Good work, so your job for pitching batting practice to 6–12 year-olds is to build their confidence through successful, satisfying repetitions.

My youth-league coach taught us that every BP should be considered a hit-and-run, which meant we were to swing at every pitch. He wanted us to learn to swing the bat. Many baseball theorists fear that approach will negatively affect strike-zone awareness—which it definitely can. But I also agree with my youth-league coach that it's important to develop in his players an interest in the game. Telling players to approach the batter's box looking for a walk is one of the easiest ways to encourage them to quit the sport. Let them swing the bat, and you can help develop their strike-zone awareness later.

Put another way, it's easier to pull the reins on a Thoroughbred than to spur a mule. I learned this lesson from a hockey coach. My oldest son, Tate, was a puck hog on the ice when he was young, and it drove me nuts. He was just learning the game, so I asked his coach, Basil McRae, if I should be encouraging Tate to pass the puck more. To my surprise, this former NHL player said he enjoyed coaching Tate and that I should "leave him alone. He's having fun, and that's the most important thing. He has a nose for the net, and I don't want to coach that out of him." I appreciated Basil for helping me as a dad following a sport I didn't know anything about, and for reminding me to let the coach do the coaching and just keep encouraging my child.

Many of the boys and their parents will want private lessons, so find out what their hitting coach is teaching them so you don't confuse the player. It's a great way to learn different hitting philosophies and help you come up with your own. Here are simple mechanics you can use as a basic template for the boys who have not had much hitting experience.

Beginner Hitting Mechanics

Balloons and Big Ball

Hit by Pitch

Just like every other skill in this game, learning to hit takes time and practice. Your goal as a batting practice pitcher should be to hit their bat every time. Start close with underhand tosses, and take your time with your arm going backward to allow them to use their natural timing. At the very early ages, a big, bouncy ball offers your greatest chance of success—see the second video.

Take the time to teach kids how to properly turn away from the pitch and you'll reduce their fear of getting hit. The third video is on how to teach a young player how to do that. Parents can do the same drill at home with a Wiffle ball or soft (foam) ball. What we praise will be repeated, so encourage players every time they properly turn away from the ball. Do whatever you can to downplay the pain. Explain the importance of on-base percentage, and make a big deal of anyone who gets on base by getting hit. We had a Bull's-eye of the Day Award that went to the player who got hit, and we celebrated their toughness.

Drills for BP Throwers

Once you've mastered throwing underhand, sit on a five-gallon bucket and dart-throw strikes overhand from a short distance away. You'll gain accuracy and your players will get the swing repetitions they need. The final stage will be to move to approximately twenty feet and hone your accuracy. See the above video on how to follow this sequence, and what it looks like to use the wall drill for practicing BP throwing, and also using a net to accomplish positive repetitions.

I favor machine pitching at the earliest ages, once players have graduated from tee ball. The machine is more consistent and there are many options. Some shoot plastic golf balls. Others shoot a soft foam ball with seams. Machines can be calibrated to the proper speed for your competition level.

As your players get older, try to mimic the release height of the pitchers they'll be facing, so they get used to the speed, distance, and angles. Whether you coach-pitch, machine-pitch, or kid-pitch, devote some of your practice time to replicating game situations.

How you finish a practice is as important as how to start it. First, on time. You've insisted on starting on time, so you owe it to the kids and their parents to end when you say you will. If you're closing with a character study, keep it crisp and interactive, getting the kids to comment or ask questions while knowing that you're going to make your points and not belabor them. Then send them off with a mention of what they can expect at the next practice.

What Stuck with Players

"First, we were to have a good attitude, proving that you want to learn, work hard, and get better. We were taught that how you practice will reflect on how you perform in a real game. You get out of it what you put into it, so we were expected to give it our all in practice. One bad attitude could change an entire team's performance."

Section Three

The Season

9

Coaching in Real Time

Once your season starts, it's all about building. You may be rotating players, letting everyone pitch, or even playing the controversial (to some) controlled games. But the key is that you're not stagnating. You have a destination. If you agree with my contention that developing responsible, contributing adults is more important than winning every game, *that's* what you're aiming for. Talk about planning for the future—producing men you can be proud of will far outshine and outlast any trophies or championships.

But let's be real and face it: a huge part of team-building, even at the youth-league level, is accomplishing something together. Building character is an *internal* goal: you want your players to know and understand themselves and what's really important in this world. The *external* goal then would be to gel as a team. Does that mean winning? Ideally, sure—but true success is measured by achieving the external *because* you've mastered the internal.

How do you manage that with all the experimenting I recommend? There are no guarantees, but here's what I believe you'll find as the kids mature over the course of the season: *Because* you're emphasizing character qualities, they'll work better together, they'll cooperate more. The best examples, those model players who exhibit the traits of the Chris Carpenters and the Adam Wainwrights I've mentioned, will be revered and followed.

That sounds like winning to me. And it's what we found with our youth-league teams. As the team developed and solidified, we started beating teams that had beaten us early in the season. The kids were still having fun, win or lose, but it was more fun to win.

So you've made it to your first game of the season. I've covered what we expect at practice, so what about during the games themselves? Preparation is key here.

Your Job During the Game

You won't have the pleasure of being a spectator. Those who believe baseball is a slow, lethargic game have never coached six-year-olds. Even if your team is older, you'll find it's like directing traffic on an anthill. There is so much to teach young players that the pace of the game radically increases.

The toughest calls for a coach at any level, but especially when the kids are old enough to pitch for themselves, will almost always revolve around pitching. When to pull a pitcher should depend on a preestablished pitch count. Pulling him because he's struggling is a completely different issue. You're going to have really good pitchers who, for a variety of reasons, simply have a tough time finding the strike zone on a particular day. If you see their confidence draining with each pitch, that may be a great time to save their arm for another day and let another boy get a chance on the mound.

One of the best pitchers on my ten-and-under team was having such a day, so we got him out quick. We encouraged him by moving him to another position and telling him that even the greatest pitchers of all time have had such days. It was a tough call, but I told him I couldn't wait to get him back out on the mound again soon.

When Kids Act Out

You'll want to establish your own rules and consequences for players who throw equipment in anger. On the one hand, you want a kid to be passionate about the game, and often that manifests by his getting angry at himself or someone else. My policy was that I would give a warning following the first offense, but beyond that I would temporarily reduce your playing time until you showed you had learned your lesson.

This was exceptionally hard for me, since the most emotional boy on my youth team was my own son. Despite his being a mild-mannered kid who loved the game—and in reality was the one of Kristin's and my five kids who needed the least discipline at home—he could lose his cool when he made an out. The first time he threw his helmet, it seemed all eyes were on me to see what I was going to do. I sat next to him in the dugout and let him know he would be benched if he did that again.

Oddly enough, he was the next to do it again, and once again, all eyes were on me. It spoke volumes to the team that I followed through on my warning, and I believe it helped cut down on that kind of thing. They knew that if I disciplined my own son, I would certainly do the same with them.

You may find, as I did, that if this happens even more with your own son, it might be wise to let an assistant coach become the disciplinarian for him during games.

Between Innings: Class in Session

It's crucial to have coaches on the bench taking notes and teaching, making sure multiple kids are listening. You'll find all kinds of teachable moments. The boys should also be taught to encourage their teammates and watch for anything that can become a competitive edge.

Trust me, you and your assistant coaches are watched all the time. If you or they are messing around, the kids will follow suit. But if someone in authority on the bench is constantly asking the boys questions about game situations, like, "What would you do if the ball was hit to you in this situation?" the boys will stay engaged. They will also likely match your energy and enthusiasm. That's leadership, plain and simple.

A player having a tough day offers you a great opportunity to reinforce your belief in them, reminding them how hard the game is and that growth most often comes through struggles. Eliminate yelling and berating. Simply have a calm conversation and ask, "What did you learn from that mistake?" or "How could you have done that differently?" Sympathy and empathy are powerful healing—and teaching—tools.

On the flip side, when a player has a great day, celebrate with them. But be careful not to miss the opportunity that too many coaches miss—helping him break down *why* things are going well. When guys are struggling, everyone seems to try everything to try to get them right. But, when guys are locked in, most people stay away, trying not to jinx the success, as if acknowledging it would make it go away.

Garbage. I recommend taking even more detailed notes when things are going well. Ask, "What is your mind on right now when you're in the batter's box?" And "What does it feel like when you grip that change-up right now?"

I would urge the guys to go home and write down exactly how far apart their feet are, the height of their hands, and any other details they can think of. They need to know what to return to if they fall into a slump. Admittedly, such information is most helpful for the older boys, but even with beginners you can emphasize, "You're catching the ball so much better. I can tell you've been playing catch with your dad and mom at home. Keep it up."

When Someone Gets Hurt

Take them off the field. If they're in the 10–12 year-old group and you've coached them for a while, you should be able to sense whether they need to leave the game or are just temporarily hurting.

For example, getting hit by a pitch flat-out hurts at any level. But you can determine whether it's a sting that will fade in a few minutes or something that might hamper their ability to run or will increase the odds of getting worse if they continue. I suggest erring on the side of caution with kids. They'll eventually figure this out for themselves and realize that most pain on a baseball field is temporary, and they'll want to stay in the game.

The opposite can be a challenge as well, however. If you have a player with an unusually high pain tolerance, keep an eye on them. When he shows any reaction to pain, be on alert and aggressive in protecting them from themselves. They'll always want to keep playing, but they probably shouldn't. A good rule of thumb with youth players is to always protect them rather than try to justify pushing a player through injury.

Dealing with Cliques

Players often settle into comfortable groups, which can be fine. But one of the biggest challenges to building a great team culture is to keep the cliques from becoming divisive. Encourage the players to do things together, and sometimes force the issue. Group certain players together in drills who normally wouldn't spend time together, or pair up unlikely partners in competitions. Such forced friendship can help expose different players to each other and keep groups from alienating themselves from the rest.

Such alienation is a form of bullying in my opinion, and good coaches simply don't tolerate this. Bullying in any form should be quickly squelched.

I once helped out with a high school team where there was an obvious separation between the more talented players and the rest. I reminded the more talented boys of the influence and respect they could gain if they used their talents to unite the team instead of divide it. Thankfully, that made a huge difference in team morale.

Bullying happens everywhere, and youth sports are not immune. If not addressed, it's a certain disaster in the waiting.

Preparation

I was advised that as a major-league manager I needed to somehow slow the game for myself, at least in my mind. I found that a well-structured game card proved priceless for game planning, game management, and for me to retain what actually happened during those hours on the diamond. My game cards helped me keep track of everything that came to mind about my players and situations and would need to be worked on with the team.

I prepared these cards well before game time, and while mine were packed with extra stats and analytics that won't necessarily apply to you, they were valuable to my decision-making process. Much of the information you may want to consider on a game card of your own, such as the following:

Pregame Information

- Your lineup—who is starting where and how they'll rotate to different positions throughout the game.
- The opposing team's lineup and any information you may have on each player.
- The name of the opposing coach and any tendencies you have picked up on them. Does he tend to send baserunners on the first pitch? Will he bunt in any situation? Does he give away his signal for a change-up (great for when you want to steal). There is always something to watch for.
- A section for WDILT (What Did I Learn Today?). Hall of Fame manager Tony La Russa told me my goal should be to learn something new every day as a coach. Even after decades of managing the game at the highest level, he continued to do that. I'm still amazed at how I can see something I had never seen before in almost every game.
- Who you have available to pitch that day, and how many pitches they're allowed.
- How many pitches your guys threw the last game, and how many days it has been since they last pitched.
- The first names of the umpires. (They prefer this to "Blue" or "Ump" or many other names not suited for this book.)

You'll likely be in a youth league that plays most of its games on the same field, and the schedule will be packed with games, several on the same day. So it's entirely unlike the big leagues, where our players would arrive at the stadium hours before the game and work their way through their personal routines even before getting onto the field for team stuff. Youth-league teams are free to arrive anytime they want, but they won't have access to the field they're to play on until the previous game is finished. There might be fifteen minutes between games, if that—hardly enough time for both teams to have infield practice and certainly not enough time for batting practice.

So you'd be smart to be sure everyone gets to the facility a half hour ahead of game time. If there's a practice diamond nearby, great, but you can't always count on that. Have your players running, loosening up their arms, practicing their jumps and steals either in the parking lot or any green space you can find at the complex. Then, as soon as the field is available, assemble down the outfield line past whichever dugout you've been assigned. While the other team is taking infield practice, your kids can be finishing their stretching, hitting Wiffle balls, or doing whatever else they need to do to get ready for the game.

In-Game Pitching

If I could give you one hint for working with your pitchers, it would be this: emphasize first-pitch strikes. Now, I know that doesn't sound like some inside secret or something fresh and new, but I can't stress this enough, especially for youth-league pitchers. You've undoubtedly heard the old pitching-count adage, "Get ahead, stay ahead." It's become a cliché, but it's also a truism that will blow your mind if you do a little research on it.

Big-league managers and pitching coaches also push getting ahead in the count, but they're usually careful not to overdo it. It doesn't take long for your opponent to catch on that you're trying to get the first pitch over to every hitter. So they sit on it and start teeing off, right? Frankly, I worried about that myself until I started studying the stats. Tracking how teams did when they started a hitter 0-1 vs. 1-0 opened my eyes to the beauty of this.

One offseason, playing in Puerto Rico, where half the players were major leaguers and the other half were double-A level or higher, I played with Los Lobos (The Wolves) in Arecibo for a coach who was absolutely determined to prove the validity of this approach. He was with a big-league organization he tried to sell on the idea of *always* throwing first-pitch strikes, and they wouldn't let him do it. They were convinced it would make them sitting ducks for aggressive hitters as soon as they caught on.

But now he was running this winter ball team, and nobody was going to tell him he couldn't experiment. He had preached the concept to everyone he knew, and he was tired of being shut down. So he told us, "I've always said I'm going to do this, and so we will." I didn't even have to signal the pitcher what to throw for the first pitch to every hitter. And I mean every hitter in every situation, regardless the number of outs, men on base, the score, anything. Every first pitch was to be our guy's best fastball, right down the middle.

Even though every other team and hitter in Puerto Rico knew what was coming, there simply wasn't a lot of success or hard-hit rates, especially early in the games. That first time through the lineup, guys were trying to get their timing down, to see what the pitcher has, and watching for that pitch in a perfect slot. When relievers were brought in with the same approach, each pitcher gave the hitter a different look. The hitters hadn't seen him yet, and he had a different release spot from the guy before him. The carry of the ball, the movement, the vertical and horizontal rotation—everything was new.

Soon the whole league knew exactly what we were doing and

what they could expect, but you would hardly believe what we saw. Pop-ups, rollover groundballs, foul balls. The hitters got so frustrated that many decided to just take that first pitch. The result? We were starting 0-1 on almost every hitter, exponentially increasing the odds in our favor.

Our coach never changed the strategy, and Los Lobos wound up winning the championship. The statistics bore out the approach, and the tactic worked.

Puerto Rican fans take their baseball seriously and follow their local teams as closely as fans in the States follow their home MLB teams. I was blown away by the attendance and support this community gave us. As a reward for winning their first Puerto Rican winter ball championship, the town of Arecibo threw a huge parade for our team. The streets were packed with people in full celebration mode. Little did I know that there was a twelve-year-old aspiring catcher in the crowd, watching with excitement and admiration as his hometown team celebrated.

That kid in the crowd turned out to be my future St. Louis teammate Yadier Molina, who well remembered that season and that parade. (He also wound up replacing me as the Cardinal catcher.) Later, when I became his manager, we were totally on the same page with that first-strike approach. It's amazing how some things come full circle. Yadi led our team for years with unparalleled game-calling.

All that to say, try that first-pitch strike strategy with your youth-league team. Imagine the advantage it will give you.

Who Plays Where?

That may appear a strange question after all the emphasis I've put on rotating players all over the field. But some kids aren't comfortable in the infield, and as long as they've given it a chance, we were happy to put them in the outfield. If one was unusually fast and could track a flyball, we'd lean toward putting him in center field.

Though I enjoyed letting lefties play catcher, second, third, and short occasionally, eventually they learned the challenges associated with that and gravitated toward first base or the outfield.

So, what about lefties playing all positions? Especially for the early developmental years, I say why not? If the endgame is teaching kids a love for baseball and helping them develop beyond the baselines, I still say: let every kid play every position on the field. Who cares if you have a left-handed catcher or shortstop? Is it fun for the kids? Then let them play wherever they want to play.

The challenge comes as the kids get into their teens and have shown both the ability to play at higher levels and the interest. That would be an excellent time for you to encourage their parents to have a good sit-down with their son and make sure it's *his* desire. A nonbiased evaluator can help evaluate the ability of the player. If both the ability and desire boxes are checked, then he can start focusing on a couple of different positions. This would be the time for left-handed players to migrate to first base, outfield, or the pitcher's mound. There are plenty of left-handed odds-beaters who have played the other positions, but the deck is stacked against them at the higher levels.

What Stuck with Players

"In my opinion, rotating positions and having everyone pitch was important. I had no idea what position I enjoyed most until I tried them all. We actually played in a huge tournament in Cooperstown where we found ourselves with no pitchers left after a long day of games. One of the younger guys finally got

> his chance to pitch, and somehow he struck out a big stud on the other team who had to be lying about his age. We still lost, but that was one of the highlights of that trip."

All Kids, Equal Innings

Along with letting kids play all the positions on the field, I strongly encourage you to let every team member play roughly the same amount of innings, no matter his skill level. I know it's hard to put a kid out there who can hardly catch a ball, but how will he learn without experience? Too many teams are happy with league rules that say everyone should play at least two innings or get one at bat. They strategize how they can follow the rule while doing the least amount of damage to their chance of winning. Fight the temptation to keep putting the kids out there who excel at certain positions. As they get into their teens and play high school ball, the best players will get all the playing time they deserve. Use your scrimmage games, controlled games, and non-tournament games to make up for the innings that less talented players may miss out on later. Have the kids list which positions they'd love to play, along with which ones they'd like to learn more about.

Coaching Third Base

New coaches are sometimes intimidated when they're asked to coach at first or third base during actual games. But this is where you have a chance to put into practice what you've been working so hard on in workouts.

Let me start with third base, because that is where most of the offensive signs will come from, and it should probably be your job as head coach. Most universities and even minor-league teams have the head coach or manager coach third base. At the major-league level, managers assign a coach to this role. It's often underappreciated by everyone else, but managers know it's laden with huge consequences and scrutiny.

For your purposes, coaching third simply doesn't have to be as complicated as it appears in big-league games. You may wonder how in the world players figure out what the sign is from all the complex motions third-base coaches go through. I won't give away trade secrets, but the fact is that most of those gyrations mean nothing until the coach flashes a trigger sign. What follows is what the hitter or the runner must focus on.

For kids, keep it even simpler than that. Kids will still miss signs. Expect that. Big leaguers miss signs all the time too. I wasn't above fining them for that because there's too much at stake if it becomes habitual. (We always designate the money to the ball club's charitable arm, but a message had to be sent to the player.) Of course you're not going to fine kids, and we've established that you won't be raising your voice at them either. But they do need to learn to pick up signs.

For the youngest players, just tell them on their way to the plate what to do. Players in the 10–12 age group can learn signs, and my team would often laugh at mine. Because I was a former big leaguer, opposing teams assumed I brought with me a complex set of signs for bunts, takes, hit-and-runs, and steals. One of my favorite sets included a rapid succession of touches down my arms, across my face, occasionally my legs and belt. Then I would clap one time for a bunt, twice for a hit-and-run, and three times for a steal. I would be talking to them while clapping, and if I clapped four or more times, nothing was on. Sometimes, despite all those contortions, if my right foot was closer to the batter that meant bunt. Left foot forward was a hit-and-run. If I walked toward them while giving a sign, regardless of what else I was doing, the steal was on.

Crazy simple, right? Well, it is. Don't complicate this. Have some fun with it.

When you're the third-base coach, you must know the game situation, starting with the number of outs. Lots of youth-league fields have no scoreboard, so it's easy for everyone to forget how many outs there are—let alone the score. Keep an umpire's count-and-out clicker in your pocket. Have your players repeat the number of outs back to you from the field on defense, but also from the bases and the batter's box. We even did this at the major-league level, despite the fact that there are at least three different spots in the stadium where the count and number of outs are prominently displayed. That's how important it is that everyone knows.

Shout, "Hey guys, one out and keep one finger in the air until all baserunners and the batter do the same!"

After you then give the signs, the first-base coach controls the runner on first, and you communicate with any runners at second and third. Say there are runners at first and third. Clarify for your runner, "There's one out and a runner behind you on first, right?" (Wait for acknowledgment.) "Run on anything hit on the ground. Freeze on any line drive, and go halfway on any flyball to the outfield unless I tell you to tag up."

I know that sounds like a lot, but the more we prepare them for, the better the odds that they'll start thinking for themselves and get it right when the ball is put into play. You will be their eyes, as they should be concentrating on the pitcher, so be aware of a middle infielder trying to pick them off. Use simple instructions like, "You're good, take another step, you're good," right up until the pitch is delivered. If you see anything out of the ordinary from the middle infielders or the pitcher or a back-pick from the catcher, shout, "Back!"

The majority of your focus will be on a runner at third, but you still need to instruct a runner at second of the game situation. I can't give you an exact age of when to start teaching all the minor details of the game, but I do urge you to push the players a little with baseball knowledge, and they may surprise you.

The following videos offer tips on various situations you may run into coaching third, such as:

1. Runner at second base only, and less than two outs.

2. Runner on second with nobody out, flyball to deep center or right field. See also the video on typical signals given to the baserunners for advancing, stopping, and sliding.

3. Runner at third and less than two outs, any ball hit on the ground.

4. Two outs, running on anything and contact play.

5. Runners at all bases, ball pitched in the dirt.

Encourage your team to watch as many MLB games as possible, and you should focus on the third-base coach. You'll be amazed at how much they communicate.

Coaching First Base

The main responsibility of your first-base coach is to be an extension of the third-base coach. The coaches should be in constant communication. The first-base coach can be an emergency backup when the boys miss the initial sign. This even happens at the major-league level, so don't be surprised when your players miss signs. A common sign given to the runner on first base will be the steal sign or a hit-and-run. The hit-and-run is a great tool used at the lower levels, as it takes the decision making out of the hands of the hitter. He must swing at the pitch no matter where it is thrown. I realize this can be dicey when pitchers aren't throwing it anywhere close. The idea is to initiate action, so this can be done only at levels where stealing is allowed.

First-Base Coaching

Base Coaching Hand Signals

Watch the first video for the things a first-base coach can do and all his responsibilities. Also watch the second video for the hand signals the third-base coach will be using, so both coaches will be doing the same thing.

Be a Good Self-Evaluator

I'm often asked the difference between big-league ballplayers and everyone else. The short answer is self-awareness. Players at the top, especially those who stay there, really understand their strengths and weaknesses and have learned to improve on their shortcomings and maximize their gifts. That's what it means to be a good, honest self-evaluator.

As a big-league manager, every spring I handed a sheet to our pitchers and asked them to evaluate which of their pitches they could throw for strikes in each possible count. Inevitably, I got a handful of responses from young throwers who claimed they could throw any pitch for a strike in any situation.

I appreciated their positive thinking, but when those same guys were on the mound attempting low-percentage pitches for strikes in tough situations, we soon had runners at every base. That overconfidence didn't help those pitchers make our team.

We coaches can oftentimes be just as poor as self-evaluators, trying to handle everything on our own. Fortunately, I had great assistants who pick up the slack for me where I was weak. I needed the organizational skills of my bench coaches to help me plan the day and get everyone where they needed to be.

I also learned to step aside and let coaches like Rusty Kuntz and others teach our big leaguers how to be Gold Glove–caliber fielders. The same thing went for our hitting coach for both the Cardinals and then the Royals, John Mabry. I can teach these skills to kids and coaches at lower levels, but pushing major-league players to the next tier, maximizing the people entrusted to my care, tested my leadership capacity. It forced me to rely on the people around me, and I urge you to be a good self-evaluator and do the same.

Bench Coaching

You'll likely find that the first actual game is when your players finally realize what the regimented practices have been all about. If they thought it was fun and different and interesting to be forced into doing something every minute and not standing around, now they realize that even when they're on the bench, they're fully in the game. Lots of coaching happens on the bench when the team comes off the field and goes on offense. But even more can happen when nine of your players are on the field and you and all your assistants are on the bench with those not currently playing.

That's where and when you can quiz players and teach them, forcing them to notice everything that's going on in the game. Every player needs to be fully engaged, whether he's on the field or in the dugout. For one thing, this helps keep a kid from feeling he's just a sub, a scrub, a bench warmer. If we coaches are doing our jobs correctly, no one should ever feel that. In fact, no one should be literally sitting on the bench, even when they're not playing. They should be up, pressing against the screen, encouraging their teammates.

Naturally, kids in the dugout would prefer to be on the field, and if they don't, they probably shouldn't be on the team. But they have a role to play regardless, and we don't involve them artificially just to try to make them feel better. There's so much to learn in the dugout, so much for you to teach.

While it's important not to overwhelm kids, depending on their age and how far into the season you are, the list of questions you can ask them during the game is virtually endless.

"What did this hitter do last time?"

"How should we pitch him?"

"If you were playing center, what would you do with the ball if you fielded a base hit?"

"How about if you caught a flyball?"

"I'm going to move the left fielder closer to the line. Why am I doing that?"

"What should the shortstop do here if a groundball is hit to the second baseman?"

Dozens and dozens of questions like that force kids to pay attention, know how many runners are on base, how many outs there are, and what the score is. At the same time, you can model what teammates should say to each other when they fail. If a kid trudges back to the dugout after swinging at a third strike out of the zone, he doesn't need to be told to "Make the pitcher get it over." He needs to be picked up. "Way to be aggressive. Get 'im next time."

One big mistake I see too many coaches make is trying to do during a game what should have been done during practice. Your job, once the game is underway and the ball is in play, is really simple. I didn't say easy. But simple. You should have the player you intended to have at each position and your lineup set the way you want it. Then you should let the kids play ball.

Your mind should be on checkpoints before each pitch, making sure the players are positioned correctly. You want to condition

What Stuck with Players

"There were times when I made an error or struck out, and all I wanted to do was plop down on the bench and not cheer the other guys on. That's when my teammates urged me to keep my head up and stay in the game. Now I know that if I had selfishly pouted, I could have hurt my performance even more for the rest of the game. We saw it in other teams when they would have a few setbacks and find themselves behind by several runs, their body language changed and they felt sorry for themselves. The way we were coached kept us from that spiraling negativity. We kept propelling each other on and never gave up, always believing we could come back and win."

them to quickly glance in your direction as early as possible so you can signal them to take a step one way or another. Even motioning an outfielder a step back when the count goes to 1-0 or a couple of steps in if it's 0-2 helps keep them engaged.

But now is not the time to coach them on arm angle, where to stand in the batter's box, how to throw, and when to swing. Maybe the reason Major League Baseball calls its on-the-field bosses managers is that they're expected to manage the team and the game, not to coach. Coaching happens between games.

Stop the Yelling!

This approach also eliminates all the yelling so common to youth-league baseball teams. Just as I push for parents not to yell during the game, I urge you not to yell either. Shouting at a player, other than to encourage him, results in a tone that can embarrass, deflate, and degrade a kid. It's even wise to have what White Sox manager (and my former outstanding bench coach) Pedro Grifol calls Tone Accountability Partners, people willing to let you know how you sound and how your voice might be perceived.

Screaming and yelling may have worked in the old days when players—particularly those who also played football—were used to their coaches communicating that way. Believe me, that ship has sailed and taken a lot of pain and scars with it. Ask yourself, "In times of stress, how do I communicate with my athletes? And why? Am I trying to squeeze out their talent at any cost, or am I truly trying to build them up as people through sports?"

Nobody likes to be yelled at, and it's the easiest way to turn kids off. Adults too, if we're honest. We coaches need to raise our voices to be heard sometimes, but watch the coach who yells all the time and see how defeated his players look. Even the ones who don't show it (of which I was one) don't like it. Make the baseball field a classroom, not the principal's office.

The first response a coach at any level may have after learning that a high-profile coach has been fired for mercilessly badgering his players is to say, "Well, I may lose control occasionally, but at least I'm not like *him*." It's easy to point the finger at someone else and forget to look in the mirror.

On this subject of yelling, imagine yourself in the most stressful situation you could possibly be in, with all of your family and friends watching. Imagine that you are asked to do something so physically difficult that most people fail three times more often than they succeed. Then imagine that the people that you respect, and admire the most in the world, are screaming at the top of their lungs at you. Sound tough?

Welcome to youth baseball. I must have grown up in a cocoon or another century (well, that's true!), but I played hundreds of games as a kid and never heard parents and coaches screaming like they do now. Maybe they feel pressured to get their kid a scholarship, or they just want him to accomplish something they were not able to do. Whatever the reason, it's flat ugly, as any kid will tell you. They have the rest of their lives to learn about pressure and stress.

I became so dead set against yelling that as a big-league manager I determined to totally subdue myself emotionally during games. I could holler at an umpire when necessary, if for no other reason than to ensure my team I had their backs. But I took to heart the idea that players should be praised in public and corrected in private.

There were times when someone would royally screw up on the field, and inwardly I might be seething, even rehearsing what they were going to hear from me later in my office. If a guy needed dressing down, I could do it, but always one on one. One of my pet peeves was any player showing up another because of an error, mental or physical. That I simply wouldn't tolerate. As for players who weren't giving their all or were making the same mistake over and over, yes, they needed to be corrected and sometimes even disciplined.

But on the field or in the dugout, I was committed to showing no emotion beyond encouraging a great play or hit. Eventually I learned that I became known for that. More than once one of my coaches would tell me what someone on the other team had asked them about me. They'd say, "Man, that guy's super intense. Is he miserable, or what's the deal?"

My guy would tell them, "You've got no idea. Mike loves the game and is having fun, but he doesn't want to do anything that would show up his players or the opposition."

The price was that I was tagged with the curmudgeon label, but I prefer to call my style bland, boring, maybe stoic. Frankly, there were opposing managers I really liked on a personal level, but it always bothered me to see them in the dugout smiling away, looking cocky. It drove me nuts. I didn't want to give them any reason to think that about me. I had a job to do, and my fun came when we walked off the field at the end of the day—especially if we won.

Scorebook

As the boys get older, learning how to keep score will help keep them engaged while on the bench and even while they watch major-league games. My grandmother listened to every Cincinnati Reds game for as long as I could remember, sitting next to the radio with a binder of her own homemade scorecards. She kept these for years as prized possessions. I didn't understand it then or know what all the numbers and letters meant, but it fascinated me.

Dealing with Umpires

I've heard that you can tell a lot about a person by how they interact with babies, the elderly, and stray dogs. Let me add umpires to that list. This may sound hypocritical if you ever happened to see me get thrown out of a major-league game (I averaged two ejections per season during my ten years as an MLB manager, but the fact is, the big leagues are different). Despite my reputation as a person of faith and one who refused to use foul language (the easiest way to get kicked out of a game), sometimes it's important for a manager to get booted. Teams want a skipper who will fight for them, argue for them, and even be willing to be ejected. A big-league manager can quickly lose the respect of his team if he refuses to mix it up with the umpires when necessary.

But don't misconstrue my actions in the big leagues as encouragement to *ever* mistreat a youth-league umpire.

Some say you should scream at an umpire early so he'll lean toward calling the close plays your way for the rest of the game. Others say to treat them with respect and kindness and they'll tend to favor you. But let's remember what we're to model here. Not shooting angles or trying to manipulate anyone. We treat umpires with respect because it's the right thing to do. Period.

Big-league umpires are highly trained, deeply experienced veterans who have been vetted through several levels before they ever officiate at the top level. Youth-league umps may have little experience as players, have been assigned to learn as many baseball rules as they can, and maybe—just maybe—sat through an hour or so of instruction. But get this: their chief qualifications are often willingness and availability. It's a thankless job that, to the best of my ability to put a calculator to it, pays roughly 3 percent of what a major-league ump receives. Naturally, pay at the highest level varies with experience, but on average big-league umps make about $1,500 a game. Youth-league umps? Fifty dollars per game if they're lucky.

Now, before I go further, I am proud to say I have had some great interactions with umpires in the major leagues, and overall I'm truly amazed at how good they are at what they do. The sad truth that you as a coach must face is that high-caliber umpiring isn't so common at the youth-league level. It just isn't, for all the reasons stated above. You'll often encounter teenage umpires who would still be playing if they could but want to keep a hand in the game this way. They are probably as overwhelmed and intimidated by their role as you are.

Just accept that you *will* have poor umpiring. The sooner you, your players, and your parents understand that, the easier it will be to handle missed calls. You should become as familiar with the rules as you can and try to help them call the game properly. But don't fall into the trap of arguing with or berating these underpaid, undertrained, and inexperienced arbitrators. Give yourself a minute to realize that they have nothing against you personally and are trying to call the game as fairly as they know how. How you handle the worst of calls will speak volumes to your team and everyone watching.

I certainly wouldn't want their job, so instead of me speaking on the topic, let a former umpire from the major leagues, who has also been a Dad Coach, help explain how this coach/umpire relationship should work. Ted Barrett came to the profession as a former basketball player, football player, and boxer and studied kinesiology at California State University, Hayward (now East Bay). Talk about someone who has earned the right to be heard—when Ted retired after the 2022 season, he had a list of accomplishments matched by few in the history of the game. He worked thirty-three playoff series (tied for most all-time), including five World Series. He served as the home plate umpire for two perfect games (David Cone's for the Yankees and Matt Cain's for the Giants), and umped third base during Philip Humber's perfect game for the White Sox—making Ted the only umpire to officiate in three perfect games.

Even during his career, Ted earned a doctorate in theology from Trinity Seminary, writing his dissertation on "An Investigation of Faith as a Life Principle in the Lives of Major League Umpires." Check out his video.

Umpire
Ted Barrett

"Hey, Blue!" just doesn't work anymore. And neither does screaming their name. Knowing people's names and using them is respectful. Even the adult veteran umps are merely human. They won't have the benefit of instant replay or official challenges, so simply accept that neither you nor your opponent should blame a loss on them.

In our youth league, if there was an older ump, I either instructed the kids to address him as Mr. Umpire or asked him how he would like the boys to address him. I was raised to not call my elders by their first names, and I coached my youth-league players to do the same.

As a youth-league coach, I instructed our players to offer no reactions to umpires' calls, emotional or otherwise. That went for me too, because I knew the kids would take their cues from the men who were to model behavior to them. I emphasized that even the very best umpires will often be wrong, let alone young umps and new ones. I was determined that we outclass every team we played in how we interacted with the umps.

Perspective of an MLB Umpire

Here's more from my friend and former big-league umpire Ted Barrett (see the QR code on the previous page). I asked for his perspective from behind the plate on how people respond from the stands. Here's what he had to say:

> My wife and I raised three children active in youth sports. We both helped coach, give rides, and provide snacks, as so many parents do. I know firsthand how much time, energy, and money goes into having children participate in team sports. But all that involvement gives no one the right to go crazy over every close play. I've seen otherwise thoughtful, intelligent, sensitive people turn into com-

plete jerks when they believe an umpire has made a bad call. I've seen umpires abused both verbally and even physically. They've been followed to their cars, had things thrown at them, and have even been threatened—all over a youth baseball game!

Much of the problem is caused by the sports media, who like to focus on missed calls and player ejections in big-league games. So we're regularly shown unruly behavior by professional athletes. But that makes it look like this is a frequent occurrence. It happens, of course, but it's rare. What we don't see is what happens most nights—professionals playing by the rules and respecting officials.

Of course, major-league players react to calls that don't go their way, but for the most part they remain respectful and don't cross the line. When they do, they are usually ashamed of their actions and seek forgiveness, which is frequently offered by the official. I had a manager who railed on me for a call one night come to me the next and say, "Hey, Ted, I thought that guy was out, but the replay in slo-mo showed he was safe. I don't know how you guys do it!"

Even when calls are missed—and I can't deny that happens—players and managers understand. They know we're human and that we have a tough job. So though they may be upset at the time, they get over it and move on.

Frankly, that needs to happen at the youth-league level too. Most youth baseball leagues can't find enough umpires. (Would you want to do it? Most think they can, but rarely do they pursue the job.) Many such leagues use teenagers to officiate games—young people with little or no training doing their best to provide kids a safe, fair game. But what do they face? Parents in the stands screaming at them and calling them names! All they want is a little fun and a few bucks, and they get vitriol from parents. And from the kids? An eleven- or twelve-year-old kid telling them they suck, or worse, cussing them out (wonder where the player got that from).

People encourage their own kids and their teammates but destroy a teenager trying to run a ball game. Face it, you're not going to get perfect umpires. At the major-league level, we are remarkably accurate, despite what the media may report. At the youth level, usually with a maximum of two umpires, it's nearly impossible to cover the entire field and know all the official rules.

How about some support and understanding for the umps? I know you want to win, but how about teaching kids the importance of being honest? I read about a player who took a new ball and made it dirty because the sun was going down and it would be harder to see. Fortunately, the umpire, the kid's coach, and his dad called him out for cheating. These days some would applaud the player and call him crafty.

I've also heard of coaches teaching their players to grab their hand and pretend they got hit by a close pitch. And if they chop a ball into the ground, they should limp like it hit their foot, trying to get the umpire to call it foul. Some call that gamesmanship. I call it cheating.

Some may say, "Well, the other team does it." I say so what? Let them cheat to win. Meanwhile, the kids you coach will learn to live honest lives. After all, would you rather raise an honest child or a so-called winner who cheats to get what he wants? The answer should be obvious.

In-Game Information

Every coach should have a pen and his own game card so he can jot down questions, ideas, and things to praise players for between innings. You might even make a note of larger, team-wide messages that should be saved for your postgame meeting or the next practice. Strive to relay information with consistency, clarity, and calm.

During the game you'll want to jot down:

- An inning-by-inning breakdown of how your players did offensively and defensively. Leave at least four spaces after each boy's name so you can note how each plate appearance went. Even a quick scorebook-style recap like E6 (an error by the shortstop), HH (hard hit), FP (first pitch) will remind you. You can develop your own codes.
- The score after each half inning, especially if there's no scoreboard and your scorekeeper is somewhere other than in your dugout.
- Pitch count for your pitcher per inning.
- What character lesson could be learned from what happened on the field today?
- What do you want to say after the game?
- Something a player accomplished that deserves praise after the game.
- What player had a rough game and could use some encouragement?
- What player needs to be corrected in private?
- What baseball rule surprised me that I need to get clarity on so I can educate the kids on it?
- Did I control my emotions?
- Do I need to apologize to anyone?

Those are just suggestions, so make this card your own, adding to it what is most important to you and deleting what isn't. The important thing is to keep with it. You may wonder when you'd have time to write all this stuff down while trying to coach a game. All I can tell you is to make the time and write in shorthand if you need to. Too much happens to remember without notes, and you don't want to miss a teaching moment.

In-Game Card

I still have almost every game card I ever filled out. Each tells the story behind the story of what really happened one day on the field. The QR code above links to one of the blank cards I had designed.

After the Game

As a coach of youngsters, your influence will mostly come after the games themselves. When the final inning ends, your team needs to show that they respect themselves, their teammates, their coaches, their parents, and the game. Postgame meetings are opportunities to drive that message home. One meeting would be with just the coaches and the players, the other—but only rarely—with parents. This can prove dicey, because parents too want to be involved in that first meeting after a game. That's why it's a good idea to have that one on the field, maybe somewhere down the line or in the outfield, beyond the parents' earshot.

It's not that we're sharing secrets or keeping anything from parents. It's just that we want to avoid any scorekeeping about who was praised or critiqued. In fact, both these meetings should be largely impersonal. For the coaches-and-players-only meeting, keep it short and don't mention individual names unless you're praising kids. Even then, be careful about honoring your stars to the exclusion of the others. If you have a couple of studs who made some great plays or drove in a lot of runs or perhaps pitched a good game, sure, that needs to be mentioned. But look for things you can applaud in everyone's play. Maybe a kid struck out three times and made an error, but he was in the perfect position to take a relay throw and got an assist on a put-out at the plate. That's worth pointing out.

If you noticed something in that same kid's hitting approach that might have contributed to his strikeouts, or if you believe he let his hitting woes affect his fielding, that's something you can discuss with him in private. Make sure any critique like that includes something specific he can do to improve on his own at home. Parents like to be included in those conversations, and the best ones will be eager to help their kid practice.

Look for character wins and make a bigger deal out of those than you do the game play itself. Mention a kid who stayed and helped clean up the dugout for the next game. Or a player who encouraged another after a strikeout. Or one who didn't overreact to a bad call by the umpire.

Generally, the meeting with the team after every game should consist of a quick overview of the game—generally what went right and what went wrong. That way, without mentioning names, you can challenge the team as a whole to do better and improve. If you made a strategic or tactical error, own it. That may lead to players admitting their own failures or missteps.

Be sure to mention hustle, energy, and effort. Even after a loss, those are the kinds of things to highlight. And keep the focus on the next game. The things you praise will be repeated. You might even choose three award winners after each game to focus on areas that have nothing to do with hits, pitching, or great plays. Those will have already likely been rewarded during the action with cheers and applause.

There's nothing wrong with recognizing a play by a less talented team member who has been struggling. Maybe a kid who has trouble with flyballs has been working on this at home and winds up making a catch that didn't necessarily influence the outcome but showed he's made progress. That's a big win for him and should be celebrated.

10

The Larger Game

Okay, so I'm old-school and don't apologize for it, but what does that mean? I can tell you this, it means a very different thing in the big leagues than it does in youth baseball. In fact, in many ways, my whole approach to the game in one is diametrically opposed to my approach in the other.

As much emphasis as I put on avoiding a win-at-all-costs mentality, especially for youth-league baseball coaches, that wasn't my attitude as a big-league player or manager. Of course I would never cheat, but I knew what my priorities had to be. You gave no inch, and your opponent was not your friend. I admired and respected most of the teams and players and managers I faced, but on game day? Not so much. I didn't want to let my guard down, didn't want to feel any sympathy or empathy or even friendship for them during the game.

I even had old friends and former teammates who would ask what was wrong or whether they had somehow offended me because I did not greet them warmly or even cordially on the field. It's a new day in baseball—and I suppose for the better—in that opposing players now show their affection and esteem for each other, sometimes even during the game.

I get it, and I know it doesn't change how they play. They're still not taking it easy on each other, always want to win, and play their hearts out. But I confess, that was not me. I know that sounds cold and maybe even out of character for a person of faith and a family man. But I was on a mission, every game, every hitter, every pitch. Whoever was in that other uniform, I wanted to beat them.

When the game was over, things went back to normal. Bob Costas even made a big deal of the fact that I showed respect to the opposing manager of the team that knocked my Cardinals out of the National League Championship Series in 2014. In his afterword to *The Matheny Manifesto,* Bob wrote:

> As his disappointed players trudged toward their clubhouse, Mike Matheny waited at the dugout railing. Waited until he could make eye contact with Giants manager, Bruce Bochy. Then, in a brief and understated moment, he lifted his cap and nodded toward his victorious counterpart. . . .
>
> You win, or in this case, lose, with class. With integrity. You play hard. You play smart. You respect yourself, your teammates, your opponents, and your craft. It's a game and it should be fun. It's a business, and those realities are there, too. But it can be more than just that. It can be, at least for some, an expression of principles.

So there's a place and a time for appropriately honoring your opponent. In the big leagues, for me, that meant when the game was done. In youth-league baseball, however, where the priority is building character, that means all the time. And it doesn't pertain just to opposing players, but also to their coaches, their fans, and even the umpires.

A Counterintuitive View of Games

If there is one unique approach I take to competition at the youth-league level, it's the one I'm about to suggest here. I have no doubt your initial reaction will be a head shake, maybe even revulsion. It's one thing to not put so much emphasis on winning, but to basically give it *no* meaning, at least at first? I know. It sounds like lunacy.

First, as I've already said, embrace games with teams against which you have no chance of winning—knowing your team will likely get drubbed, even dismissed after a few innings by the massacre rule. But I'll go a step further. See if the opposing coach will allow you to keep playing even *after* you're down by ten or twelve runs. See if they'll play their second string, allow position players to pitch, and let you experiment with your lineup too.

But second, and even more importantly, if yours is the team doing the dominating, stop the game, let the umpire know what you're doing, and tell the other coach to play the rest of the game, allowing his entire team to bat around each inning, regardless of the number of outs. He can even let his bench players hit. Maybe, with no limit to the number of outs and giving a dozen or more hitters a chance, they'll scratch out a few runs. But what if they come back and beat you? So what? The kids—all of them—will have fun. And they'll learn that winning isn't everything.

Believe me, this will be a hard sell to most parents and fans. "Aren't you even trying to win?" they'll ask. Well, there's a time and a place for winning too, but it's not when the teams are so clearly mismatched. Let the kids play. Let them have fun. Let them learn.

The best part of this approach comes later in the season when you again face a team that put a beating on you. Because your kids have grown and improved, all the while learning character and sportsmanship, they might surprise you by upsetting the very team that smashed them early.

Obviously, you don't try this strategy without fully informing the parents. Besides thinking you've lost your mind, unless you explain the reasoning behind it, they might think of taking their kids elsewhere to play. Such a strategy has to have everybody on board.

Communication with all the parents is crucial, especially before the first game of the season. Some, without having completely thought it through, may have expressed agreement with your new, unique philosophy of coaching. Are they really prepared to be largely silent during games? Maybe they thought you meant only that they shouldn't berate their child or correct him if something goes wrong or he strikes out or makes an error. That's a given, of course, but you may have to hammer home the point that for some kids, even shouting encouragement makes them shudder.

That's probably the most controversial part of my coaching philosophy—urging parents to be silent during the game. Naturally, I can see why many would question what could possibly be wrong with hollering, "Let's go, Johnny! You can do it!" And maybe they're right—depending on the kid. Perhaps some kids do need and want that kind of encouragement, but my counsel is to urge parents to find out in advance. Advise them to have a sit-down with Johnny and ask him straight out, "What do you want to hear or not hear from me during the game?" Many will be surprised to hear that Johnny doesn't want *any* attention during the game. There's pressure enough if he's pitching and every eye is on him. Or if he's a position player and all the attention shifts to him when the ball is hit or thrown to him.

Most of all, many kids feel self-conscious and conspicuous when they come to the plate—whether they're leading off an inning, coming up with no one on, or have runners aboard and driving them in will make the difference in the game. Yes, some unusually self-confident players can tune out distractions. Some may even enjoy the attention. But you'd be surprised how many simply want to do their best, not have their name called out, not even be encouraged. I've coached many players like that—good, confident athletes who just want to concentrate on doing their jobs.

Now, if a parent has had that heart-to-heart with their kid and he's okay with a little applause and a "Go get 'em," that's fine. But if—and as I say, this happens more often than not—he prefers that his parents not say anything, by all means, they should honor that request.

That goes for you as the coach too. I've seen too many coaches try to micromanage every plate appearance. Maybe you've heard them. Or maybe you've been that coach. "Move up in the box! Raise your elbow! Watch for the breaking ball! Level swing! Eye on the ball!" It's like the old joke about the golfer who stands over the ball, trying to remember the book he's just read, *93 Things to Remember at Tee Off.*

I have a friend whose son was a gifted catcher as a ten-year-old and took a foul tip off the mask. The umpire rightly stalled a bit, brushing off the plate, trading out the ball for another, and so forth. But he made such a show of making sure the kid was okay, the catcher started crying, which brought out his coach. "You all right?" the coach asked him.

"I just want to play!" the kid said.

He was more upset by the attention than by the foul tip.

So clarify with the parents that you're not just trying to prohibit embarrassing kids with criticism or correction, you're trying to eliminate *all* attention to them that they don't want.

Controlled Games

It's just as important that parents are up to speed on scrimmages, or what I refer to as controlled practice games, or else you might face a mutiny of sorts. Sometimes it's obvious even before the game starts that one team is significantly advanced over the other. That's the time to get together with the opposing coach and suggest a controlled game, wherein either coach can stop it at any point and do some teaching.

That may sound bizarre, especially to uninitiated parents, but let me give you an example. With John Mabry as one of my assistant coaches, our youth-league team faced a team the same age as ours but who clearly had not had the experience or training we had. Before the game I suggested to the other coach that John and I would be willing to teach his team a few things, if he was interested. Which he was. So we cleared with the umpire that on occasion we might call time-out just to do that.

Early in the game, we got a couple of runners on and our next hitter drove a ball into the gap. The other team pretty much stood watching as the outfielder chased the ball to the wall and then heaved it toward the infield as hard as he could. It bounced and rolled and a couple of infielders nearly knocked each other over trying to get to it. By then our lead runner was rounding third, with the second runner right behind him.

Had the shoe been on the other foot, we would have waited until the opponent's runners scored before we stopped the action, but in this case, to prove we were doing this for the benefit of both teams and not just ours, we stopped our runners and called time-out. Then John and I showed the other team where everybody should have positioned themselves when that ball was hit—where the relay men should be, who's backing up whom, and how to get that ball in as quickly as possible to minimize the damage.

It's a no-brainer that both teams learned a bit, as did our other assistant coaches and the opposing coaches. Now, you may not feel you have enough baseball experience to do that, but if you do, try it and see the goodwill it brings about. In that case, we left our runners on base, though they would have easily scored, showing that we were all about playing fair, being good sports, and teaching all the kids a few things so they'd have more fun.

Needless to say, you don't do that in every game, especially later in the season when you're in tournaments or playing more competitive teams. But you can see that there's a time and a place for controlled games.

I also enjoyed it when we faced younger or smaller teams, and I could see they were more gifted than our kids. My team would be thinking that their opponents looked like their own younger siblings and fully expected to easily beat them. What a great lesson to be humbled by such teams!

Likewise, as I've said, it can be thrilling to develop a team capable of beating a squad that looks bigger, stronger, and faster and who might just also have all the latest equipment in their designer bags.

Blowouts

Every team, from tee ball to the major leagues, gets destroyed now and again. It happens. Your ace may have an off day. Errors might pile up on you. The other team gets hot and everybody's hitting. Before you know it you're down by ten runs or more. Believe it or not, there's a lot to be learned from that kind of ordeal.

First, the question becomes when or if you give up. You can imagine my response to that. Never. Even if the game appears hopeless—and probably is—you, as good sports, owe it to your opponent to keep battling. Make them earn it, even after the outcome has become a foregone conclusion. In the big leagues, no, you wouldn't pitch your ace reliever late in a massacre like that—unless he needed the work. You have to be smart and think of the next day's game and how your bullpen stacks up for the rest of the series.

But in a youth-league game, there comes a time to gather the whole team in a circle. Maybe the scoreboard shows the hopelessness of their coming back. Ask them, "Is anybody done? Anybody ready to give up and quit?" If you've been teaching character and running them through tightly scheduled drills in practice, you're likely to hear, "No way!" Get them to commit to giving it their all the rest of the way, regardless of the outcome.

It's rare, but I've seen miraculous comebacks in games just like that—at all levels.

Sportsmanship vs. Ignorance

On the other hand, there is the matter of how badly you should beat a mismatched team. Some years ago a story emerged of a girls basketball team that defeated its opponent 161–2. Imagine. One of the comments I read said that the only people who have an excuse to run up a score like that are professional teams—those getting paid to play. I strongly disagree. To me, massacring an opponent like that shows a blatant disrespect for other people, not to mention for the very sport they're playing.

Running up the score and rubbing your opponent's face in a loss disrespects everyone in the game, including the winning team. I know some win-at-all-costs proponents—in business and in sports—will call me soft, or a loser, for saying something like that. So be it. I'm going to assume that you, as a youth-league coach, know what's the right thing for your team. Almost without fail, coaches who run up the score have some sort of agenda, and it's the opposite of what is best for the kids. Maybe it's personal—a grudge, a statement, some sort of payback—or perhaps it's simply pursuing that ever-alluring trophy. Jerks can always rationalize ridiculous behavior.

Unfortunately, even youth leagues and tournaments tend to reinforce this by rewarding teams who blow out opponents in a game that's abbreviated by a slaughter or massacre rule, as if this were a greater feat than simply winning. Points are awarded teams that produce greater run differentials, and teams are encouraged to massacre their opponent so they can save their best pitchers for the finals. Well, maybe that's one way to plan your game according to the rules. But we all know there's another set of rules, characterized by doing the right thing because it is the right thing.

Even at the major-league level, where millions of dollars are on the line and no one is going to voluntarily surrender a win, there are unwritten rules that keep teams from disrespecting their opponents and the game. A couple of times each season, a team will find itself on both sides of this issue. Most handle it the right way. When my team built a huge lead, certain things just had to stop. We stopped stealing bases. We quit trying to bust up the close play. We didn't swing away on a 3-0 count. And we didn't let our guys spin themselves into the ground on huge swings. We stopped celebrating openly, because we knew that tomorrow the shoe could be on the other foot. There were even times when we had a big lead and a runner on third base, a wild pitch went to the backstop, and we held up the runner.

So, yes, even in a game where careers and millions of dollars are on the line, we know what the right thing is to do. So as a youth-league coach, what's at stake for you is the character of your players. If you find yourself in an out-of-town tournament where your team is simply much better than the rest of the competition, have your entire team work on hitting from the opposite side of the plate. And don't let them make it obvious by making a mockery of it and laughing about it. Just tell them to do their best while hitting from the other side.

This is also when you can bring in the player who rarely pitches and give him a shot. Maybe move your right fielder to shortstop even if he is left-handed. I'd like to think that if I were that dominating girls basketball coach I would have had my team dribble and shoot only with their weak hand, or have to make seven bounce passes before being allowed to shoot.

A basketball ref told me about a game he worked where one team started the second half with a fifty-point lead but still had all five starters in and were running a full-court press. During a timeout the ref asked the head coach if he was really going to keep this up for the rest of the game. The coach said, "My team needs to stay sharp, and I don't believe in ever holding back."

To his credit, that ref told the coach, "You're basketball-ignorant, hurting the kids on both teams."

It all comes down to motive. If your motive is to dominate and embarrass your opponent just to make yourself look better, then you've even moved past sports ignorance. You're just plain ignorant.

Simply be creative in those situations and you can continue to work on improving your kids' skills while still respecting their opponent. What if the other team begins a comeback? Good! Who cares? What's more fun than a close game that challenges everyone? You can always revert to your original game plan. Simply do the right thing.

Participation Trophies

The idea that everyone is a winner may be good during the earliest years of organized sports, but there is too much to learn from losses and failure to let kids think that everyone should get a trophy, even when they come in last place. Someone wants to protect the psyches of kids and encourage them all, especially if they lost almost every game of the season. I agree they need to be encouraged, but not with some phony trophy that implies they won something. If they need encouragement, encourage them! Tell them how they improved, developed their skills, became better people. Celebrate growth. But reserve trophies for the kids and teams who have worked the hardest to develop their talent, come together, improved the most, and won.

This may seem counter to my emphasis on developing character over the idea of winning at all costs. But when you get into the actual season, of course the point of each game is to win. No, not by shortchanging some players by having them play less because they're not as good as some others, but certainly by emphasizing the fundamentals and doing things right. While the occasional parent might say they wish you cared as much about winning as other teams seem to, you can assure them that you do—but not at the expense of good sportsmanship.

But the fact is, in real life there are winners and losers. And while, no, you don't want to label a kid a loser just because his team didn't succeed, don't pretend. Kids on losing teams who get trophies anyway don't value those trophies. They know better and they probably feel compelled to tell anyone who sees their trophy the truth that they got it just for participating. Want a kid to learn to compete and excel in life? Make him earn his trophies.

There's nothing wrong with letting kids see their shortfalls and encouraging them to figure out ways to fix them and jump right back into the fight. Even big leaguers' skill sets did not come to them before they faced losses, and failures. We need to allow our young athletes to fail so they can develop perseverance, goal-setting skills, and a true work ethic.

Excellence vs. Perfection

Everybody knows that baseball is not a game for perfectionists. Perfection is so rare in baseball that perfect games are celebrated for how extraordinary they are. Do a web search on how many perfect games have been thrown in the major leagues since 1900, then divide it by the number of games that have been played since then. Next, search for how many unassisted triple plays have been turned in the history of baseball. Finally, how many immaculate innings? That's when a pitcher throws 9 consecutive strikes, without even a foul-ball strike after the count goes to 0-2. These feats are so rare that they become phenomena to talk about for days afterward. No one expects such perfection or realistically sets out to accomplish one of these feats. Imagine all the luck that has to attend such successes.

Any player with an ounce of self-respect strives for excellence—the best you can hope for in a game full of failure. Everybody knows that most players with long careers who can maintain a .300 batting average are likely to be inducted to the Hall of Fame. But that also means they have failed to get a hit in 7 out of 10 plate appearances. As a manager, I loved it any time one of my teams flirted with winning 100 games in a season. But in a 162-game season, even that means we failed to win 38 percent of the time.

At all levels, it's simply accepted that you can do everything right—especially as a hitter—and still fail. Maybe you hit a screaming liner, even harder off the bat than a typical home run, but right at the shortstop. The scorebook says you're zero-for-one. You can only hope a Texas Leaguer (a weak pop-up) somehow eludes the defense. What should have been an easy out is now on the hit side of your ledger.

That's why excellence, rather than perfection, must be the pursuit. You can be excellent and still fail, which teaches mental toughness if nothing else. The question is how you handle failure. Of course some people fear success too, and as weird as that sounds, it can be a valid worry. What if they're praised for their accomplishments but feel they were just lucky? They might suffer imposter syndrome, where they believe they've been only lucky and are waiting to be found out. Some also worry that success will go to their head and spoil them, make them someone they're not.

The best thing we can teach kids pursuing this game replete with failure is character traits that will carry them through both failure and self-doubt. I'd rather see a kid grow into adulthood having faced some heartbreaking losses than having succeeded at everything he set out to do. That's not real life. Life throws you curves, knocks you down, roughs you up. Facing that as a youngster can make you or break you.

That's where the actual games come in—the measure of a person is not determined by their successes but by how they respond to their failures.

11

Is the Coach Always Right?

Well, Yes and No

Unfortunately, we have too many recent examples of people in leadership who have perpetrated unspeakable crimes against kids. That makes it all the more important for parents to be extremely careful about who they entrust their kids to. Stories of trusted coaches now spending the rest of their lives in prison—and their unimaginably damaged victims—are heartbreaking, sobering realities.

As a coach, you must make it a major part of your overall mission to not only keep everything aboveboard between the coaches and the kids, but to also make it impossible for anyone to even imagine otherwise. It might sound like overkill, but parents deserve the peace of mind of knowing that safeguards are firmly in place. Establish rules of how many kids or adults will be together (and where and when), and enforce those rules.

Once you have guaranteed that every kid is safe, it falls to the other parents to take responsibility for supporting the coaches influencing their kids. One of the greatest lessons my parents taught me was that my teachers and coaches are always right—even when their individual decisions may have been wrong. It goes without saying that there are moral and criminal exceptions, as I mentioned above. A coach choosing to spend time alone with a player other than his own kid, showering him with gifts or attention, is inappropriate—and dangerous—on the face of it.

But with all that being precluded by your strict rules of behavior, players should be taught to respect and honor their coaches and realize that they have the right to be wrong. You're human. You'll make mistakes. Your strategy may be faulty, meaning that sometimes you'll suffer a bad outcome. Sometimes you'll luckily benefit when you shouldn't have. In either case, you were wrong.

I know there were times my parents felt I was not treated fairly by a coach, and it had to hurt them. But you know what impressed me about them? I never heard them talk negatively about any of my coaches or teachers. And they didn't allow me to criticize them either. I know my parents kept up to speed on what was going on and what was being said, but they never badmouthed the adults in charge of me. And now I'm glad they didn't. I had my own negative thoughts and ideas, and it wouldn't have taken much to encourage my cynicism. As I say, sometimes my assessments were accurate. But Dad and Mom didn't allow that, and the parents of your players shouldn't either.

Grateful as I am that I was taught respect for authority, you may find parents who look for every opportunity to jump down your throat when something doesn't go perfectly for their child. Imagine what this teaches the kids. I've seen players hop from team to team every year in search of the perfect coach. As you'll soon learn, if you don't know it already, there is no such thing as a perfect coach. It's better for parents, and their kids, to learn that quickly. It's so easy to defend our kids and voice our disapproval during the car ride home after the game or at the dinner table. But if we do that, how can we expect our kids to not do the same thing?

The truth is, life is at times unfair. How we handle that can set our kids up for success or failure, depending on the course we choose. As a coach, be prepared to recognize the teaching opportunity here. Maybe a parent or a player comes to you with a complaint. If they're respectful and seem willing to listen, acknowledge it if you have made a mistake. If you must defend your decision, do that with deference and respect too. The Bible says that a soft answer turns away wrath, and you don't even have to be a person of faith to test that.

A friend of mine tells the story of a neighbor kid who was shouting insults at his own son over the backyard fence. His son asked his dad for a few insults he could hurl back. Rather, Dad said, "Try this instead. Tell him that no matter what he says or thinks, you still want to be his friend."

His son tried that, and voila, the boys were soon playing together again. It works.

Clearly, in the course of our coaching, we *will,* at least unintentionally, occasionally wrong the people entrusted to us. That's the time to go out of our way to ask for forgiveness and make things right. A true apology carries no "But if only . . ." We're tempted to say, "Maybe I shouldn't have said this or done that, but if only your son hadn't . . ." Apologies are all about *your* fault. Own it and deal with it. You might be surprised at how often a parent, or the player, will thank you and acknowledge their part in the problem too.

Taking a Time-Out

Many parents have asked me what they should do when their son seems to have simply lost his passion to play. It isn't fun for him anymore. Here's an easy answer, though it may be difficult for parents to apply it: let the player take some time off and just be a kid.

Too often, we want our kids to pursue *our* dreams for them. They may start out wanting to please us, but soon they fall prisoner to staying on that course. I can't tell you how many players in the big leagues took time away from the game at some point in their development. Some were convinced they were done and would never return to baseball. But obviously they *did* return, and that temporary break could very well have been one of the most important reasons. Had someone forced them to keep playing, their next time out might have been permanent. Fortunately, they had adults in their lives who were wise enough to let them take a break.

There's a temptation to remind an aspiring young athlete that he survived a pressure-filled tryout, that his friends and relatives would be disappointed if he took a season off. There are too many stories to ignore what happens when kids burn out of a sport. But there are just as many stories that prove kids can take time off from a sport and not just return to form, but also often come back even better—motivated and excited.

One of my players in the major leagues—fast-tracking toward a successful career—was so hard on himself and so overwhelmed by the expectations he allowed others to place on him that he finally had to take a break from the game. He got a regular job, which gave him time for some soul-searching. He soon realized that he had never taken a break from baseball before and wasn't prepared for the grind on the path to stardom. The break proved to be exactly what he needed, and he returned to the game with a revived sense of purpose that was all his, not something pressed upon him by others. He enjoyed a long and successful career.

One of my own sons, at age twelve, told me he didn't want to play youth-league baseball anymore but wanted to pursue another sport. I think it shocked him when his mom and I quickly supported his decision. But we did insist that he personally tell his baseball coach during the winter, when the coach had time to rework his roster. My son made the "grown-up" phone call and felt relieved to be pursuing only one sport.

Full disclosure: I did call the coach later and asked him to keep a spot open on his team if at all possible, in case my son regretted his decision once baseball season rolled around. Sure enough, that's exactly what happened. My son rekindled his love for baseball and begged the coach to allow him back.

I do think we made the right decision in allowing him the break—if only in his own mind and only temporarily. I wonder what would have happened if we would have made him keep playing because he was so talented. Would he have eventually quit? Who knows? He went on to set all kinds of baseball records at his high school, played at a Division 1 college program, and wound up playing six years of professional ball.

At some point the game needs to become a kid's own, and that can happen only when they feel the freedom to walk away from it if they aren't enjoying it. I confess that's the perspective of a father who almost got it wrong. We just need to be careful with these young psyches.

The Role of Faith in Coaching

As I've tried to make clear, this is a book about coaching and not my personal faith, though I don't apologize for it. You may share my beliefs and values, or you may not. I hope you'll still find value in what I've learned over many years in the game and in the dugout.

You may recall that in my letter to parents several years ago, I included a section that dealt with faith and sports. While I am admittedly outspoken on this topic and strove to not waver from it as a big-league manager or a youth-league coach, I don't want you to cringe or skip this section—even if you bear scars from negative religious experiences. I completely understand that you may carry resentment due to very real harm inflicted on you by others who claimed a personal relationship with God. All I can do is apologize for that—and for them—and hope you'll hear me out. I deal with people every day who may have experiences similar to yours.

I also, however, believe I'm obligated to be forthright about my convictions and to live up to who I say I am. Responsibility comes with claiming to be a Christian, and part of that is to not be ashamed of it just because it may no longer be politically correct to be vocal about one's faith. First, I would simply ask that you not jump to generalizations about Christian believers. While, regrettably, you may have reason to believe we're all the same—because some who identify as people of faith can be closed-minded, maybe even bigoted, racist, anti-women, far right-wing, etc.—trust me, that in no way defines me or true biblical faith. My faith is about a relationship with Jesus Christ, so if you're determined to judge me, judge me by how I live up to His example—not how some others who call themselves Christians might.

So, what does this have to do with coaching? We've all seen people who wear their emotions and passions on their sleeves and try to tell everyone what they should believe and how they should live—whether anyone is interested or not. I may admire the boldness of someone like that, but it's simply not who I am. I've told every team I've managed or coached that I will never try to force my faith down their throats or hold them to the same expectations I hold for myself. I will, however, not shy away from an opportunity to talk with them if they have raised the subject or have questions. It is an honor to be able to walk through life with the guys I've coached.

However, as we've established, life is not always fair, and troubles are unavoidable. If we coaches are doing our jobs the way that I believe we should, sometimes conversations come up that go much deeper than batting slumps and sore muscles. That's when I have the opportunity and feel the freedom to share my own life experience, which happens to include a God component. I could take the easy, more comfortable way out and cower from the truth for fear of being accused of political incorrectness, but I don't. I want to live in such a way that my life speaks louder than my voice ever could. I hope to share what I believe by how I go about my daily business and how I treat others. I resonate with what St. Francis of Assisi said: "Preach the Gospel at all times, and when necessary, use words."

When Adversity Strikes—and It Always Does

Adversity can either paralyze or motivate. Every team faces setbacks. The question isn't *whether* you will face one, but *when* you will. What are you going to do about it? Players get injured. Players get traded. Players become disgruntled. Do you as a coach turn tail and run? Give up?

Naturally I hoped and prayed that my teams, at every level, could stay healthy and intact. But they rarely did for long. A coach is judged not by how he leads during the mountaintop experiences, but by how he manages the valleys. I would urge you to plan ahead, expect adversity, and determine in advance how you'll respond to it. Refuse to let adversity change your focus or turn you or your team into victims. A real victim is one who suffers unjustly or truly has no options. As long as you have choices, there's a way forward. But once you have surrendered to adversity and allowed it to paralyze you, a downward spiral begins that is hard to recover from.

I want to tell you about one of my heroes, a man who faced adversity eye to eye (literally) and used it as motivation to persevere. But first let me share that one of the many things the

St. Louis Cardinal organization has done well for a long time is to include its player legends in spring training and even during the season. Imagine the immeasurable impact of the presence of people like Stan Musial, Bob Gibson, Lou Brock, Ozzie Smith, Bruce Sutter, Whitey Herzog, Tony La Russa, Willie McGee, Red Schoendienst, and others. When I got the manager's job in 2012, one of the first things I did was to contact each of them and ask them if they would join us for spring training. Almost to a man, they wanted to make sure I knew they wanted to be more than just hood ornaments, as Bob Gibson called it. They loved our fans and enjoyed interacting with them, but they wanted to be around the players and in the clubhouse only if they had a purpose and were truly wanted.

"Are you kidding me?" I would ask them. What team on the planet wouldn't want a cast of baseball icons in their camp? Gibson actually told me that he didn't think many of our players would even know who he was, and he was serious. The truth was, we were all starstruck, especially by him and Stan Musial, but of course by all of them. I will never forget getting a congratulatory video from Mr. Musial the day I got the job. I have that priceless recording saved in multiple places and made sure each of my kids have it saved also.

But back to the hero who epitomized overcoming adversity. If you're looking for someone to emulate as a coach and, even more importantly, as a man, here's your guy . . .

Red Schoendienst

If you're too young to recognize that name, pronounced SHANE-deenst, it's my privilege to bring you up to speed. He's been gone since 2018, dying at age ninety-five, but right up until his passing, I absolutely loved spending time with Red. He was cool as anyone

I know, period. In fact, he may be the most incredible athlete I've ever seen, but it was *who* he was that impressed me more than *what* he accomplished. Talk about a guy who faced adversity . . .

He was raised in Illinois, not far from St. Louis. His father was a coal miner with seven kids and the family had no running water or electricity. Red proved so good in baseball as a youngster that he forced himself to hit left-handed in school to keep things fair. He dropped out at age sixteen and took a job with the Civilian Conservation Corps. Working on a fence, he took a nail to his left eye and was so severely injured that doctors recommended removing the eye. Red found a doctor willing to try treatment other than surgery, but he suffered terrible headaches for years during rehab.

After that, Red told me, he found it difficult to pick up breaking balls batting right-handed against right-handed pitchers. So in those instances he became a switch hitter, reverting to batting left-handed as he had as a kid. In the spring of 1942, he attended a Cardinals open tryout with about four hundred other players and was eventually signed to the D-level minors. To say he started fast would be an understatement. He got eight hits in his first eight at bats and hit .407 in six games. He quickly rose through the ranks of the minor leagues but was drafted into the army in 1944. He was soon medically discharged due to trauma from shooting bazookas. The Cardinals invited Schoendienst to spring training in 1945, and he led the National League's second basemen for seven seasons. His 1956 league record fielding percentage of .9934 held up for thirty years.

Red was eventually traded to Milwaukee, where, in 1957, he and Hank Aaron led the Braves to their first pennant in nine years and their only World Series title in that city.

During the offseason Red suffered from tuberculosis and underwent a partial pneumonectomy. Despite being told that he would never play again, he rejoined the Cardinals in 1961 and eventually became a coach and then the manager. The Cardinals retired his No. 2 in 1996.

After I finished playing for St. Louis and before I got the manager's job in 2012, I had been fortunate enough to be able to spend time with Red away from the field. We both had a passion for the great outdoors, and Red hardly missed a day of duck season, and even more rarely missed a duck. Even at ninety he could drive a golf ball 250 yards. I know it's a cliché, but with Red, it's true: they don't make 'em like that anymore.

He often texted me and would always introduce himself this way: "Hey, Mike, this is the old Red Bird . . .". I loved getting those messages and still have them saved on my phone. One that stands out is when I got the job and he asked, "Do you still want me around?" He was completely sincere. I about fell over and quickly called him to assure him I absolutely did still want him around. He once called me during that first season to tell me he was going to be a little late getting to the field because of a doctor's appointment and asked if I would be okay with that. He said he could change the appointment if necessary. Imagine. That's just the kind of man he was.

When I managed the Cardinals from then until 2018, Red showed up at spring training every season, in uniform, from the time he was eighty-nine years old until he died. He eventually became special assistant coach, and the year before he passed he completed his seventy-second consecutive season as a major-league player, coach, or manager. Imagine my privilege to have Red Schoendienst as a special assistant.

What I most appreciated about him was his humility. Here was a guy who accomplished as much or more than just about any player in baseball, so I often tried to get him to address the team. But he always politely declined. Red was good, however, about having the right individual conversations with the right people at the right time. He spoke quietly and gently in such a way that it never sounded like he was trying to force his ideas or opinions on anyone. He insisted they were just suggestions to take or leave, but let me tell you, he reminded me of the old E. F. Hutton TV commercials. When Red spoke, everybody listened.

He enjoyed talking to the players about how much the game had changed since he broke in. During his playing days the team had only a couple of fields on which to get in all their work, and no batting cages. He said each player would usually get only about twenty swings a day, if they were lucky. Our guys could only shake their heads. They were getting in two hundred swings before breakfast.

No wonder Red considered playing pepper so important. Besides practicing the basic skills of hand-eye coordination the fielders needed to handle groundballs and bad hops to either side, the hitter also developed bat control. I'll never forget Red, in his eighties, playing pepper with two of my sons and hitting the ball wherever he wanted, no matter where the pitch was. He was the kind of a teacher who enjoyed demonstrating more than talking. His classroom was the baseball diamond, and he liked to teach while wearing spikes.

Red was always watching. He could be four fields away and notice a player do something specific. In typical fashion, he rarely offered unsolicited comments on the things he saw, but he always had an answer if I asked him about one of our players. Then he would tell me something that impressed him, positively or negatively. Our team photographers sent me many photos I cherish of Red and me behind the bullpen mounds, evaluating pitchers.

Red would share how he used to build a pitching staff, admitting it was pretty easy when Bob Gibson and Steve Carlton were in the rotation. His real passion, however, was for infielders. He could sit and watch them all day long. He enjoyed working them out too, hitting beautiful grounders with a fungo bat, which appeared to be just an extension of his arm. He could put the ball wherever he wanted and even call out how many hops it would take to reach the fielder. Of course we had other talented infield instructors, but Red's evaluation carried a lot of weight with me. I trusted him implicitly.

Experience, wisdom, discernment, humility, and unwavering loyalty were qualities Red Schoendienst brought not just to the baseball field, but also everywhere he went. I loved that man. What an honor to sit with him just days before he died. Some legends keep teaching long after they are gone, and that was Red. I will always miss the Old Red Bird and his commitment to helping me develop as a player, as a manager, and as a man.

Stan the Man

A lot of Red Schoendienst's stories involved his best friend, Stan Musial. The two seemed inseparable teammates and roommates during the golden age of baseball. Red would praise Stan for how he always kept signed baseballs in the trunk of his car to hand out to boys playing stickball in the streets, or how they would drop in with no fanfare to visit sick kids at local hospitals.

Red and Stan were wired similarly. Musial appeared more dazzling in the public eye and is numbered among the all-time greats of the game, but both displayed quiet strength and confidence and were known for stellar character.

Section Four

The Postseason

12

When the Game Is Over

The Broader Lessons of Baseball

That you're still with me tells me we're on the same page when it comes to what's really important in the lives of the young people you're coaching. As it's unlikely you'll see one of your players becoming a professional in any sport, remind yourself that what happens during the majority of their lives will occur not on the baseball field. Real life is lived between games and practices during the season, between seasons, and after their playing days are over.

Your role as a coach doesn't stop just because you're not running drills every few days or managing a couple of games each week. Now is the time to double down on those moments when you can really impact your former players in the larger game of life.

Offseason Practice

If you *are* still coaching, naturally there are practical baseball matters to attend to as well. I recommend allowing a certain amount of throwing, but not too much too soon in the winter. The QR code on the following page links to an example of an offseason

Offseason Throwing Program

throwing program for older boys. Older teams might bring in a hitting coach or even a pitching coach. There are good instructors in most areas in the US who charge by the hour and may be worth investing in to take a look at your boys' mechanics. The winter offseason is usually a good time to take advantage of such expertise, and often the cost can be spread out among all the players instead of paying for individual lessons.

Meanwhile, take advantage of the opportunity to impart lessons to the kids that apply to baseball and to life. Such as:

Lesson 1: Motivation

I often told my big-league clubs during spring training that we don't automatically become a team just by wearing the same uniform. We have all seen ball clubs on paper that should run away from their competition, only to pull in different directions on the field and fail. Unfortunately, Major League Baseball fosters a selfish model because players are not, for the most part, compensated for what they do as a group. Individual statistics determine their next contract, not so much the number of games their team wins.

My first year as a big-league manager, it became immediately obvious that times had changed. When I was a rookie in the Milwaukee organization, some of the veterans told the spring-training batting-practice pitcher to take it easy on them since they hadn't picked up a bat all winter. Nearly a decade and a half later, I could see that modern players didn't waste their offseasons. They showed up in shape and ready to go, knowing how important it was to their careers and their wallets.

Red Schoendienst told me he used to sell shoes in a department store during the offseason. Can you imagine that now? When Nolan Ryan came up with the Mets in the 1960s, he had to drive a gas truck in the offseason to make ends meet.

But besides all I told you about Red Schoendienst above, what blew me away was that he remained a stellar model to this generation of players. With Red nearby, it was easy to send a message to our guys that they should control what they can control. I'd tell them that if they put in the work, they could look back with no regrets. "Work hard, work smart, and let your talent take over." I reminded them that they are always being evaluated and to not let anything get in the way of their dreams. "The window of opportunity in baseball is small. Don't allow some foolish decision keep you from getting to the big leagues after you've come so close."

Lesson 2: Friends

Something I've strongly promoted to any ballplayer, from youth league to the major leagues, is to choose their friends wisely. In fact, this was a subject we often referred to during our character studies. You don't want players learning the hard way that friends can either make us or break us. Better to model forging friendships in the fire of serving others. Get your kids to define their friendships and determine whether the people they choose to hang with make them better people and point them in the direction they dream of going. It is a hard truth, but if they are not willing to sever ties with the so-called friends who drag them down, they are lying to themselves about how badly they want to achieve their goals.

Try this visual demonstration I used even with big leaguers: I stood on a chair in the middle of the clubhouse and asked whether it would be easier for me to pull a friend up onto the chair with me, or for my so-called friend to pull me down. It becomes immediately obvious that the latter is easier.

So, how to develop constructive friendships? I've found that teams who both play and work and serve together stay together and engender the kinds of quality relationships that can last a lifetime.

I realize that you're not likely to have an opportunity to do the following with your team, but one of the most eye-opening experiences I have ever had came when my coaching staff and I got to visit the Naval Special Warfare Unit training center in Coronado, California. There a group of potential Navy SEALs were in their second week of seeing whether they had the right stuff to join that elite team. You may know that any candidate can give up, surrender, and drop out, but they have to publicly ring a bell to announce that fact. As you can imagine, this is the last thing anyone wants to do. But by the time we got there to observe—on day two of week two of a four-week weeding-out course that challenged their minds as much as their bodies, thirty-five candidates had already rung the bell, deciding it wasn't for them.

The remaining group was pulling themselves off the beach, carrying their rafts. If they made it through the four-week trial, they still had to endure one more weeklong test. They would be allowed just four total hours of sleep during those seven days—two hours on Wednesday and two on Thursday. All this just to be one of the select few honored with the SEAL name.

We spent the day talking with veteran members of SEAL teams, and it quickly became obvious that there was something different about these men. They displayed both humility and genuine love for their teammates and their country. I spent time with one gentleman who had served on multiple SEAL teams and had been a leader and an instructor. I asked what were the characteristics he saw in those who made it through the process and were selected. He told me there are five things such men have in common:

- They must be physically tough. (He said this is the easiest of the five qualities to find.)
- They must be mentally tough.
- They must be morally tough. (He described this as doing the right thing, all the time, even when nobody is looking.)
- They must believe that the needs of the team are greater than their own needs.
- And they must be humble.

That's a great list, no matter how you slice it. What does this have to do with baseball and coaching kids? It simply reinforces the need for you and your assistant coaches to help parents raise high-character kids. They may not be destined for the SEALs or the big leagues, but they just might make a difference as a businessman, a dad, a husband, a citizen.

Build that kind of atmosphere on your team and model it to the best of your ability.

It's a rare treasure when some of your best players become also your hardest workers and the most "others-centered" people on your team.

But often, personal priorities challenge the ability to function as a team. Issues come up, and even big leaguers often have to make tough decisions—like whether to tend to their families or stay with the team. The right thing is almost always to put their families first, and this is also a dilemma that many youth teams face. It takes dedication and commitment to keep a good team together, but too many teams swing the pendulum too far the other way and don't allow families any room to enjoy their summers together.

As a coach, remember that kids have summer breaks for only a few years, and they need the freedom to make lifelong memories with their families—sometimes away from baseball. That means occasionally you'll lose a player or two to family vacations. Try to have alternate kids on your roster who can fill in when necessary, and ask the parents to inform you of their summer vacation plans early. That way you can schedule tournaments and games around the dates when multiple families will be gone.

Community Service

If the term *community service* sounds too much like something a criminal is forced to do as part of his sentence, feel free to call it *service projects.* Getting your team to see the value of serving others, serving their community, basically offering themselves to help others however and wherever they can, is the best way I know of to bring your character studies to life. It's one thing to model selflessness before the kids or spend a half hour of every practice session talking about it. It's quite another to lead your team to act on it.

There's no substitute for getting your players involved in hands-on service to others.

While you're focusing on having your team doing the little things right and becoming fundamentally sound and disciplined, start planning now to get them thinking outwardly. I've spent a lot of time here trying to teach selflessness, but it soon becomes time to put this to the test by putting it into action. Physical and mental toughness can overcome a lot of bad influences. But regardless of how I may feel, I have the option of not letting those influences affect how I invest my day and how I impact people. You and I can talk all we want about the importance of putting others ahead of ourselves, but we had better be careful to practice what we preach.

It's easy to serve others when we know we'll be rewarded for it.

But are you and your players willing to sacrifice and do for people who might never be able to pay you back? When you do, you'll find you gel more than ever as a team. I told my big-league teams that we walked into spring training as sixty individuals with no guarantee that we would develop into a team. That happens only once we start functioning as one and looking out for each other—not to mention serving our fans and others less fortunate than we are.

So what can your team do to start thinking outwardly and putting others ahead of themselves? Just ask your town council or Chamber of Commerce or any community service organization what they need help with, and you'll get more suggestions than you could use in a lifetime. Maybe a nonprofit needs yard work done, for which they can't afford to pay a landscaping company. Is it mowing their lawn, raking leaves, trimming bushes?

Does someone need a storage shed cleaned out, garbage taken to the dump?

Does a senior-citizens center need visitors to read or just chat with its residents? They love interacting with people of an entirely different generation.

No question, some of your players may resist this at first. Maybe they're not expected to do laborious chores at home. Or maybe they've never been comfortable interacting with senior citizens beyond their own relatives. But what can be more character-building than nudging them outside their comfort zones? They'll quickly learn the truth of the adage that it's more blessed to give than to receive.

One of the most rewarding efforts our youth-league teams took on is what in our area was called Challenger Baseball. It may go by a different name in your town or you might even have to organize it yourself. But it's simply this: baseball for physically and mentally challenged kids. Often such children are taken to watch youth-league or even big-league games, but perhaps they can't walk. Or if they can walk, they can't run. Maybe they don't have control of their limbs or muscles.

What your team will learn, the first time they try what I'm suggesting here, is that those kids have the same dreams and aspirations of anyone else their age. They're not fooling themselves that they'll ever be able to run and catch and throw and hit or steal a base or slide across home plate. But they would love to emulate their favorite big leaguers or able-bodied friends they've seen play. They would enjoy putting on a uniform. And what they'd *really* enjoy is being out on a baseball field themselves.

So find such a group in your area and invite them to a real baseball field where those kids can get out on the field and even walk, or be wheeled, or use their crutches to move to their favorite position. Pair one of your kids with each one and let the game begin. When the ball is hit anywhere near one of the challenged kids, help them field and throw it. Some of them will come to the batter's box in wheelchairs. Some won't even be able to hold a bat. So one of your players can swing for them and then push their chair up the baseline.

You won't believe the mile-wide grins of these kids who have always dreamed of this. And trust me, your players will never be the same after they've seen the joy they can bring to others.

An International Trip

You should be able to tell from the title of this chapter that I'm heading somewhere else with summer plans. Not every team or individual family will be able to afford an international trip, but the rewards will be unforgettable for those who can. If your team decides to do it, you may have to conduct a lot of fundraising to include as many players as you can. But we decided to take our youth-league team to the Dominican Republic for two very specific reasons. First, we scheduled games against local teams down there, so yes, it was a baseball trip—and our kids were excited to compete. But second, we also went to serve. There were socioeconomic areas in the DR unlike anything our players had ever dreamed of—let alone seen with their own eyes. We let it be known that we would be there to serve, to help, to work on all kinds of building and maintenance projects.

That was the best part of the trip for me—watching our kids' eyes grow wide learning how valuable their efforts could be. It also quickly became obvious which of our players were the most mature about such things. Some wanted to hold back and observe and play the role of star players, doing as little of the actual work as they could get away with. Others, sometimes wholly surprising us, jumped in with both feet, not only working tirelessly in the hot sun, but also befriending the locals. One of our kids—and frankly not one of our most talented players—emerged as a natural, especially with younger kids in the neighborhoods. Despite the language barrier, he warmly greeted everyone and had fun with them, even hoisting little kids on his back and giving them rides.

I confess I got a kick out of our team—which by then had become pretty accomplished and used to winning a lot back in the States—getting beaten regularly by the DR teams. I mean, you talk about the difference in cultures . . . We never became that team with all the expensive equipment and uniforms, the kind we so enjoyed beating in our simple T-shirts. But now here we were where even our meager equipment was so much better than theirs. It looked like a bunch of ragtag neighborhood kids cobbling a team together to face Americans who seemed to have anything they wanted. And you know what? More often than not, they whipped our tails.

Full Disclosure

To be completely transparent, I must confess that years before this I had to have a transformation in my own character when it came to the Dominican Republic. During my early years in professional ball I was assigned to play in the DR during the offseason, and I frankly wasn't excited about going. It wasn't that I thought I was better than the players—or anyone else—from there, but I had had some run-ins with some Dominican players in the States, and I allowed that to paint them all with the same brush. That's to my shame, of course, but it took my going there and playing there and experiencing the culture to get my mind and attitude right.

Twenty thousand fans would show up for those offseason games, and talk about passion. Not only did it seem they lived and died with every pitch, but even on the way to the games we never passed an open field that didn't have kids playing pickup games. I learned quickly that for many kids in the Dominican, the options were limited.

By the time I left there after that one season, I had been changed—changed in how I thought about Dominican players and about the nation itself. I had a greater appreciation of the game itself and how they played it, and I was able to start over and really connect with my Dominican teammates in the United States.

You can imagine what a privilege it was to expose our youth-league players to the DR. I didn't have to say a word. They saw at very young, impressionable ages what I had seen as a budding pro player, and I know it deeply impacted them. By the time I took another group of boys down there, I was managing the Cardinals, so we brought in our young pitcher, Carlos Martinez. He showed our kids the home he had grown up in—corrugated tin held up by wood poles. He told them that when the rains came and the river rose, they had to move everything they owned into the rafters of that hut to keep it from floating away.

GO Ministries

I know our kids will never forget that, and neither will I. It was everything I hoped it would be and then some. If you're interested in a similar trip, I suggest starting your fund raising years in advance. Contact GO Ministries in the Dominican Republic to learn more.

What Stuck with Players

"Such service projects were some of the most impactful moments in the whole ride with our team. The DR trip was one of the most defining moments in my life. It opened my eyes to the world around me and put everything in perspective. Aside from being a blast, that trip was so unique that if it was possible, I'd urge every youth league to try to do it."

Another says, "The DR trip made me appreciate everything from being able to play baseball to our style of living. The kids down there often played the game with bottle caps if they didn't have a ball, while we complained about a ball with a scuff on it. Our parents always told us to appreciate what we had, but I don't think I really did until I saw how other people were living."

13

Winning the Long Game

Your True Reward

I understand that not everyone agrees with my opinions, and that is all I have to offer: opinions. But I'd like to believe that my views are relatively educated ones, not because I'm some youth sports guru, but because I'm nothing if not curious and eager to learn. That means I ask a lot of questions, especially of the people I've been privileged to rub shoulders with—those who do this baseball thing for a living. Hopefully our ideas have been of help to you. I hope you'll take advantage of every one of those.

I trust by now you have gleaned that, while I'm thrilled for my youth-league players who went on to play at the collegiate or professional levels in baseball, hockey, or any other sport, helping get them that far was not even on my radar until they showed prodigious skill as they got older. The point up till then was for them to have fun and to build character. Ironically, without those two elements, not even their talent would likely have propelled them that far.

As I have been hammering away at from the first page, only one in a million kids will go on to play at the highest levels, so there is much I added so your players become wholesome, valuable contributors to society. That's the long game, the one you really want to win. That's why I've saved till the end those things I urge you to ponder during the offseason and, again, when your coaching days are over.

Transitioning from Coach to Mentor

You may have accepted your Dad Coach role with modest expectations. You'd help out, teach the kids a few things, and let them have fun. Someone has to do it, right? I hope by now you can see that the ultimate benefit—not just to the kids, but also to you—can be far greater and long lasting.

Before I close with several examples of why I feel richly blessed after having coached kids and taught them character, let me offer a few personal tips you can employ while you're in the middle of coaching.

Stay in Your Lane

A bit of advice that served me well and might serve you too came from one of my favorite big-league players to watch over the years, now working in the White Sox front office. Jim Thome may be one of the most respected and talented players to have ever played the game. The first time you meet big Jim you have to wonder if it's possible he could be for real. Could a former Major League Baseball player really be that nice and genuine? Well, it's no act. Jim was a fierce competitor, but off the field he's a model of how we should all treat people: with class and respect.

I once called Jim in the middle of a season when his team seemed caught up in daily fights in the clubhouse and controversy in the media. The talk of his town was about everything on that team but baseball, but Jim never seemed to be in the middle of it, despite his seniority and leadership position on the team. I asked him how he managed that.

He said, "Mike, I just stay in my lane."

How simple, yet profound. He was doing his best to help his team through the adversity, but he refused to become emotionally involved. He wanted nothing to do with that lane.

So that's my challenge to you. When you make decisions parents aren't happy about and they resort to gossip, just remember that parents are always emotionally involved when it comes to their kids. Stay above it. Be a peacemaker. Stay in your lane.

Handling Criticism

This isn't easy, I know. No one likes to be criticized. The fact is that there will be people unhappy with you no matter how great a job you do. That's unfortunate, because yours is a volunteer gig, and you don't need—or deserve—the hassle. But the kids need you. That you are still with me this late in the book tells me you're wired the right way to make a strong, lasting impact on the boys entrusted into your care.

One of the things I never completely mastered was handling the criticism that came daily with managing in the major leagues. I mean, I handled it, but not as well as I could have or should have. I am a pleaser by nature, so the haters irritated me more than I like to admit. The new adage is that haters are going to hate, and I was eventually able to develop a crust to all the negative input. Had I not, there's no way I would have lasted ten years as a major-league manager.

The danger comes when that crust you create turns into you into a generally crusty person. That, I never want to become. I admire the honesty of singing star Mariah Carey, who said in an interview that she can hear a thousand praises and just one criticism, but the criticism drowns out the thousand praises.

As a Dad Coach you won't hear anywhere near a thousand praises, but you're likely to hear a lot more than one criticism. Focus on the good you're doing for your boys, and just do the next right thing.

Find a Mentor and Be a Mentor

By now you know how deeply important it is for you and your assistant coaches to encourage growth not just on the field but in the everyday lives of the kids entrusted to you. I hope I've served as a bit of a virtual mentor for you within these pages and the videos and that you've found my colleagues serving that same role for you.

Even better, if there's a man in your orbit who can continue serving as a mentor to you, that's hard to top. Anyone farther down the road of life from you who has proven to be successful as a husband, a father, a confidant, or a citizen has much to teach you, if he's willing. And it'll soon be time for you to serve in that capacity for the kids you're coaching now.

I can't emphasize enough how quickly these kids will grow up and start having kids of their own. Now is the time to hold team events or even small dinners with a player or two or a player and his parents, just to see how things are going. You'll find that this means the world to a kid.

Thank You

I'll finish by letting more former youth-league players recount their experiences. They are the proof of the pudding and can say it better than I can anyway.

What Stuck with Players

One remembers that during the offseason "we would meet with the coach individually to discuss our baseball goals, but also with our life goals as well. Those conversations and the characters studies helped us mature and envision a future that others our age were not even thinking about. We knew they would always be there for you as role models who cared more about us as people than as baseball players."

Another says, "It has to be extremely rare in youth sports to have that kind of support and balance. On the one hand they coached us. On the other they let us figure out a lot of things on our own, teaching us to think and make wise decisions."

Another says, "What sticks with me is that we were taught true sportsmanship, which included treating umpires with respect and playing the game the right way all the time every time."

And finally, another says, "Challenger baseball, where we gave the physically and mentally handicapped kids a chance to play, changed my life. I was just a kid, but I would leave those games with a full heart. To see how much they love life and appreciate everything really made me put my own life into perspective."

These kinds of memories from kids you've coached is what being a Dad Coach is all about, and it's what I want for you. Thank you for taking up the mission. If you have stories to share, or feedback or questions for me, I'd love to hear from you.

Former Player Testimonies

Acknowledgments

Thanks to the coaches who taught me more than just the sport:

Ron Golden, Dave Starling, Bill Freehan, Bob Humphreys, Del Crandall,

Tim Ireland, Chris Bando, Phil Garner, Dave Ricketts,

Dave McKay, Dave Duncan, Tony La Russa, and Dayton Moore.

I am indebted to my personal board,

M.H. (Mike), R.A. (Rick), D.G. (Derek), D.T. (Denny), R.C. (Ron), M.M. (Mack), J.K. (Jeff), S.H. (Scott), P.N. (Paul), amazed at your willingness to serve so selflessly.

"Thanks be to God for His indescribable gift!"

(2 Corinthians 9:15)

About the Author

Mike Matheny is the author of *The Matheny Manifesto,* played thirteen years as a catcher for four Major League Baseball teams, won four Gold Gloves, and holds the MLB record for most consecutive chances at the position without an error. He was the manager of the St. Louis Cardinals for six seasons—leading the Cardinals to the postseason in each of his first four campaigns and winning the National League pennant in 2013—and the Kansas City Royals for three seasons. He has appeared on *Fresh Air, Good Morning America, Fox & Friends,* and more.

Jerry B. Jenkins is the author of twenty *New York Times* bestsellers. His writing has appeared in *Time, Reader's Digest, Parade, Guideposts,* and dozens of Christian periodicals.